KU-190-804

BEASTS
AND
SAINTS

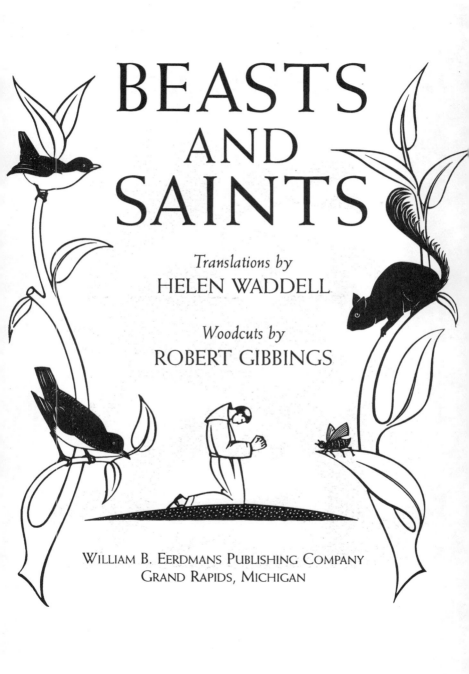

BEASTS
AND
SAINTS

Translations by
HELEN WADDELL

Woodcuts by
ROBERT GIBBINGS

WILLIAM B. EERDMANS PUBLISHING COMPANY
GRAND RAPIDS, MICHIGAN

Translations © 1934, 1995 Helen Waddell
Introduction © 1995 Esther de Waal

First published in 1934 by Constable and Company Ltd/
The Macmillan Company of Canada Ltd

This edition first published in 1995 by
Darton, Longman and Todd Ltd, London

This edition published 1996 in the United States of America
through special arrangement with Darton, Longman and Todd by
Wm. B. Eerdmans Publishing Co.
255 Jefferson Ave. S.E., Grand Rapids, Michigan 49503
All rights reserved

Printed in the United States of America

00 99 98 97 96   5 4 3 2 1

Library of Congress Cataloging-in-Publication Data

Beasts and saints / translations by Helen Waddell;
edited by Esther De Waal.
p.   cm.
Translated from Latin.
Originally published: London : Constable and company, ltd., 1934.
Includes bibliographical references (p.).
ISBN 0-8028-4223-2 (pbk. : alk. paper)
1. Christian saints — Biography.   2. Christian saints — Legends.
3. Animals — Religious aspects — Christianity.
4. Desert Fathers — Biography.   5. Celtic Church —
Biography.   6. Christian saints — Ireland — Biography.
I. Waddell, Helen.   II. De Waal, Esther.
BR1710.B43   1996
270'.092'2 — dc20
[B]   96-16346
                         CIP

CONTENTS

THE SAINTS OF IRELAND

CONTENTS

TRANSLATOR'S NOTE

THESE are stories of the mutual charities between saints and beasts, from the end of the fourth to the end of the twelfth century. They are translated without sophistication from the original Latin, most of it of the same period: the detail of the actual sources will be found on the last pages of this book. By restricting these sources to Latin, I have had to forgo the race of the vernacular; Robert Mannyng's bear who came to keep a lonely hermit in company, and as he came up to the gate louted and made fair cheer— 'Feyre chere as a bere myght': the four Irish scholars who went to sea for the love of God and took nothing with them, only that the youngest said, 'I think I will take the little cat': the grasshopper who came to Portiuncula through a winter's night to sing the midnight office for St. Francis, and left his small tracks in the snow, to the compunction of the slothful brethren who had lain warm in their beds. The truth is that the Middle Ages are so rich in this kind of story that without some arbitrary principle of selection one is hampered by too much liberty. Choice is difficult enough even in Latin, though here it has again been limited to the pre-Franciscan saints. St. Gerard's wolf that was bidden to impersonate the calf it had killed, and came and stood meekly before the distracted cow to her great satisfaction, till it wearied of this quiet life and suborned a young deer to take its place: St. Karilef's bison that came to him to be petted and scratched between its horns; these and a score of good monsters have been omitted, together with the lions who dug a grave in the desert for Paul the Hermit, and who still weep wide-mouthed and dig on their capital at Vézelay, more movingly even than in St. Jerome's prose. But Jerome's *Vita Beati Pauli Eremitae* is too subtly constructed to be mutilated for the sake of a single episode, and must be translated in full in some other place.

[ix]

St. Jerome indeed makes no appearance as author in this
collection, though he shares the title-rôle with his Lion and
his Donkey in its most considerable story; a story that throws
an unusually mellow light on that scholarly and irascible saint.
The manuscript that records it is not earlier than Xth–XIth
century: there is the gravest suspicion that Jerome acquired
his lion by confusion with St. Gerasimus, a less distinguished
and more genial abbot a little higher up the Jordan, whose
lion and donkey were a good deal less sophisticated than the
animals of the later version. Erasmus spoke of it disdainfully
as a fable unworthy the merits of so great a man, and even
the grandmotherly benevolence of the *Patrologia* admits that
it is without gravity, and pieced together *ab inepto sarcinatore*.
Yet how the 'inept botcher' enjoyed his tale, and his own
preposterous prose: and how humane a figure is his *saepe
praedictus pater*, his already frequently mentioned saint. *Hunc
tamen ne exasperetis* – 'Do not nag at him' said Jerome simply,
when the brethren were blaming the lion on circumstantial
evidence only. This is not the Jerome that Rufinus knew:
but it is the Jerome that Carpaccio knew, and endeared to
Christendom on the walls of San Giorgio di Schiavoni. Here
is the benevolent old man who leads his lion into the cloister,
while the affrighted monks swoop like swallows to their eaves;
here is the lion that paces, affable and ingratiating, behind
him: and here, impassive and self-sufficing to the last, is the
donkey who crops the herbage in the cloister garth while
Jerome dies in the foreground, and the lion rends heaven with
his bootless cries.

It was Jerome's sometime friend Rufinus who is responsible
for the story of the Blessed Ammon and the Dragons. It is from
the *Historia Monachorum in Ægypto*, the tale of a journey
undertaken by a party of seven persons to visit the monks
and eremites of the *Thebaid* in the winter of the year 394. It
is not certain that he was one of the party: but the book was
either written or translated by him for the brethren of his
monastery on the Mount of Olives. He was given to grunting

a little in his speech, so that Jerome unkindly called him
Grunnius: lavishly hospitable, a trifle luxurious in his tastes,
and a hearty admirer of asceticism in others. A similar
account, the *Historia Lausiaca*, was written in Greek by Palladius, a friendly, inquisitive, and much journeying monk,
who held St. Jerome's scholarship and venom in equal awe,
but was a staunch disciple and lover of St. John Chrysostom.
His experience of the desert stretched over the last ten years
of the century, but the book was not written till 420, when
the wanderer had become a bishop. His story of St. Macarius
and the Hyæna is the only extract taken not from the Latin,
but from the infinitely more spirited Coptic version translated
by Amélineau.

Most of the stories of the Desert Fathers were translated
into Latin from their original Greek, during the fifth, sixth
and seventh centuries. St. Pachome who summoned crocodiles
to ferry him as one calls a cab from a rank, died, a very old
man, about 405, and his life was translated in the sixth century
by the abbot Dionysius Exiguus, so called not because he was
a little man, but because of his great humbleness. St. Simeon
Stylites, himself the most dragonish of the Saints, converted
his dragon sixteen years before his death in 460; his life was
written by Antonius his disciple. The story of the Unsociable
Lion, a very rare instance of grudging hospitality, comes from
the *Verba Seniorum*, translated by John the Subdeacon, pos-
sibly he who succeeded Pelagius in St. Peter's chair in 599;
while the story of Gerasimus and the Lion is from the *Pratum
Spirituale*, written by John Moschus, himself familiar with
the desert, about 620.

Yet the most fragrant of these stories, *The Hermit's Garden*
and *The Penitent Wolf*, are from a Latin original. They were
told to Sulpicius Severus by his friend Postumianus, just off
his ship at Narbonne, after three years journeying in North
Africa: the two sat together on their cloaks, Postumianus now
and then hitching his a little nearer. The *Dialogus* which
records that conversation is one of the earliest instances of

the idiosyncrasy of French prose, although the words are Latin: and the pages of it are haunted by a gracious ghost, the Abbé Brémond of blessed memory, so near a neighbour in birthplace though so far divided in time, and master, like his predecessor, of a gay and gentle irony. Sulpicius was a barrister of Toulouse, friend and contemporary of St. Paulinus of Nola: like him, he was fortunate in birth and ambition and friendship: and like him, renounced the world in his prime. But a kind of exquisite worldliness kept with him, a sidelong glancing wit, and a way of writing prose that runs like water. The *Dialogues* were probably written about 405, a few years before Sulpicius died in 410, the year of the sack of Rome. His friend Paulinus survived him, and Rome, for another twenty years.

Of the Saints of the West, *The Death of King Teudiric* belongs to that century and country about the Severn Sea, which is the matrix of the legend of Arthur and the last fight with heathendom. It is embedded in the *Book of Llan Dâv*, among charters and boundaries, its purpose there being to explain the possession by the bishops of Llandaff of the lands about Mathern, free of tax or impost to any secular man, inasmuch as Mouric gave the earth upon which his father died to St. Oudouceus, Bishop of Llandaff, and his successors in the see, for ever. St. Oudouceus died early in the seventh century: the book was compiled in the twelfth: but the story, like its more famous counterpart, has the quality of time-lessness.

The next two legends, *St. Columba and the Crane*, *St. Columba and the White Horse*, are rooted in a craggier soil: they are the gentlest things recorded of the heroic and tempestuous abbot who founded Iona. The *regio nostrae paternitatis*, the countryside where he and his crane alike were fathered, is Gartan in Donegal, at the ingoing of the mountains and the great lake; a gentle countryside, and more apt a birthplace for the bird that came flying, buffeted with wind, and fell exhausted on the western beach, than for that other precipitous spirit. The life, written about 690 by Adamnan, also an Irishman, and himself abbot of Iona, is a rugged piece of work: but the death-days of the Saint, and the crowding torches that discovered him dying in the dark before the high altar at midnight of the 9th of June, are one of the tidemarks in medieval prose.

The life of Columbanus, 'Prince of Druids,' founder of Luxeuil and Bobbio and a Rule of passionate austerity, was written by Jonas, a monk of his own abbey of Bobbio, some time after 640: Columban himself died in 615. St. Malo, the saint of Brittany, died three years after him: his life was written five centuries later by a quiet scholar, Sigebert of Gembloux, about whom, said his admiring disciple, there was always an air 'of antique knowledge and reverence.' The stories of St. Cuthbert are from the life by the Venerable Bede: they show in little the quality not only of the saint of the Farnes but of his biographer: the historian's care to note source and authority: the quick eye that had observed how a horse crops and pulls at the hay above its head, and how a sad bird trails its wings: and an even narrative prose that can deepen to a solemnity that is, in his own phrase, *undisonus*, its sound like the sea.

St. Werburga and the Wild Geese, on the other hand, is William of Malmesbury in his voice of cheerful gossip, narrating a local miracle: the abbess died about the year 700. Benno, Bishop of Meissen, was a spirited saint (he died at a great age in 1106) who took the precaution, before obeying a summons to Rome, of bidding two trusty canons lock his cathedral doors in case of trouble and throw the keys into the Elbe: whence they were recovered, under the fin of an obliging fish, upon its astute bishop's return. His life was written in 1512 by Jerome Emser, a Doctor of Canon Law, author of a dialogue as to whether potation is to be tolerated in a properly constituted State, and of tracts against the more spiritual intemperances of Luther and Zwingli. One observes the agreeable Renaissance pedantry with which the over-loquacious frog is bidden to be a Seraphian, inasmuch as the frogs in the island of Seraphus are mute, and can but admire the ease with which the frog, knowing his Pliny, was able to take the allusion. St. Godric of Finchale is with Bartholomew of Farne (*ob.* c. 1193), the most recent of the saints: he died about 1170, at a great age. He was a Norfolk man, a pedlar, and then took to sea and became a ship's captain: he may be the *Gudericus pirata* who carried Baldwin to Jaffa in 1102: at any rate, though he died far inland, he would to the end of his days be troubled on stormy nights for ships at sea. He was a pilgrim to the Holy Sepulchre: and coming out of the waters of the Jordan, and looking down at his feet, ' *"Lord," said he within himself, "for love of Thy name, Who for men's salvation didst walk always barefoot through the world, and didst not deny to have Thy naked feet struck through with nails for me: from this day I shall put no shoes upon these feet." '* It is the accent of the liturgy, the poetry of plain men. He kept his vow to the end: and his biographer and younger contemporary, Reginald of Durham, knew him go barefoot through the frost, peering under hedges for such small animals as might be helpless with the cold.

The last section, The Saints in Ireland, derives from the collection of saints' lives in various Trinity and Rawlinson MSS. edited by Plummer in the *Vitae Sanctorum Hiberniae*. The story of St. Kevin and the Blackbird is from Giraldus Cambrensis: the Fly who would keep his place in the codex for St. Colman is from Colgan's pleasant seventeenth-century prose, retelling in Latin the legends which 'Ketinus' (Joseph Keating) had already collected in Irish. The others are probably the work of Irish monks as late as the twelfth century, yet they are in some sort the most archaic of all, both in the simplicity of the narration and the untroubled acceptance of the ancient understanding, that one finds in folklore, between man and beast.

'Here one would take

[xiv]

A fox and one a deer for acolyte,
And fresh from night
The hawthorne brake
With you gave thanks in scent and song for light.'[1]

Except Ciaran of Saigir, who is made contemporary with St. Patrick, the saints belong to the sixth and seventh centuries. St. Ciaran, founder of Clonmacnoise where the kings are buried,

> 'Battle-banners of the Gael, that in Kiaran's plain of crosses
> Their final hosting keep,'

died in 549: St. Brendan of the Voyages in 577: St. Cainnic, abbot of Aghaboe, in 599: St. Colman mac Duach in 611: St. Kevin (Coemgann) of Glendalough in 618: St. Moling of Ferns in 697.

'Marvellous' – it is Colgan's meditation on the good offices of St. Colman's fly – 'are these condescensions of the grace of God . . . yet how befitting His loving-kindness that those who have renounced all fellowship and service of men . . . should themselves receive the good offices of dumb beasts and a kind of human ministering.' Yet the Saints have had no monopoly of the kindness that is between men and beasts. Homer pitied the crying of the sea-birds when the village folk have stolen their unfledged young from the nest: and old Argos on the dunghill, full of fleas, wagging his tail and dropping his ears at the sound of Odysseus' voice, but unable to drag himself nearer for old age, is the most moving thing of its kind in literature. Plutarch was eloquent on the 'native magnanimity' that he found more often in beasts than in mankind: and he is never so engaging as when he describes the elephant that knew itself more stupid than the rest of the troupe, and was found one night rehearsing and 'conning its lessons' by moonlight; or the hedgehog who goes through a vineyard

---

'Robin Flower: *Peregrinari pro amore Dei* in 'Poems and Translations' (1931).

laboriously impaling grapes upon its little spines, till finally, itself a walking bunch of grapes, it bends its steps towards home and the regaling of its family: or the horn-owl who so admires the rhythmic dancing of men that it watches them in an ecstasy, humping its shoulders and jigging on its perch, and lo, the fowler creeps up behind and takes him unawares. It is a hard heart that will not lament him, or that will not contrast 'the lovely friendship and civil society of pismires' with that of politicians. Boethius, himself in prison, wrote half a dozen lines on a wild bird caged in a cellar that sprang too high and saw the waving trees, and how thereafter it spurned its seed and its honeyed drink with small indignant claws.

'And all day long it pines for the green leaves,
And whispering "the woods", it grieves – it grieves.'

Twelve centuries later Swift opened his cupboard door to put coal on the fire, after Patrick was gone to bed; 'and there I saw in a closet a poor linnet he has bought to bring over to Dingley . . . I believe he does not know he is a bird: where you put him, there he stands, and seems to have neither hope nor fear.' St. Malo would not move his cloak, because a wren had nested in it: and the other day a professional in a golf championship let go his chance of it, because he would not play his ball out of a thrush's nest.

For if the dark places of the earth have always been full of the habitations of cruelty, there has always been a spring of mercy in mankind. The Roman virtue of *pietas* is the strong root from which our pity, in every sense, derives. Religion has had its own savageries: yet even the arbitrary Godhead of the Book of Job was concerned for the young ravens wandering from the nest for lack of meat, and it was Christ's claim that a huddle of feathers on the ground was not unregarded by the Father of mankind. 'With Christ,' said Sulpicius Severus, 'every brute beast is wise, and every savage creature gentle': and St. Kevin refused the levelling of the mountains about

[xvi]

TRANSLATOR'S NOTE

Glendalough to make his monks rich pasture, because he would not have God's creatures disturbed for him. In the first paradise that lies behind the memory of the world there was no cruelty: and when Isaiah, sick of war, made his poem of the golden world, the climax-vision was a holy mountain where 'they shall not hurt nor destroy.' And whether these ancient ways of thought seem to us only the delusions sloughed by a wiser world, or whether

> 'those first affections,
> Those shadowy recollections . . .
> Are still the fountain-light of all our day.
> Are still a master-light of all our seeing'

it matters very little.

> 'For still the heart doth need a language, still
> Doth the old instinct bring back the old names.'

The beasts have still their way with us: Dürer's hare looks out on the world with his timid confiding; and the gentlest of the gods still has in his armoury

> 'a twilight air
> That can make anchorites of kings.'

INTRODUCTION

THESE stories of saints of a distant past and their relationship with the creatures around them make delightful reading for any of us, of whatever age. They are entertaining and charming, giving gentle, often amusing, glimpses of a world in which men and women moved easily and naturally with the wild creatures, enjoyed their company and their friendship, loved them and nurtured them and in return gained much from their company and their support. There is no doubt at all about how vivid they are, what beguiling reading they make, how they immediately attract us with their attention to detail, to snatches of conversation, to the unguarded thought.

We meet here a range of creatures, from lions and hyenas to a mouse, a fly, a frog. Some are immediately attractive – the otter, the stag or the hare; others, such as the sow, the wild boar or the frog, are rather less so. Yet all, whether they be huge or small, beautiful or not, are as it were here given their own voices. When St. Benno is praying and he finds that his prayer is disrupted by the croaking of a talkative frog in its slimy waters, he first commands its silence but then, thinking that perhaps this singing might after all be agreeable to God, 'issued his command to them, that they should praise God in their accustomed fashion: and soon the air and the fields were vehement with their conversation' (pp. 65–6). There are poignant moments, such as when, knowing that the saint is soon to die, a white horse, his faithful servitor who used to carry the milk pails, puts his head on St. Columba's breast and cries, his tears running down into St. Columba's lap, 'and he foamed as he wept' (p. 45). There are entertaining moments, such as the backsliding of the fox who, tired of the vegetarian diet that his life as St. Ciaran's 'first disciple or monk' involves, abandons his vow, steals his abbot's shoes and carries them off to his ancient dwelling in the forest planning to chew them there, and how the badger is sent after him to bring him back to submission and repentance (pp. 94–5). There are charming moments, as when at Glendalough St. Kevin is deep in prayer with hands outstretched and a blackbird settles there and lays an egg, and 'in all patience and gentleness he remained, neither closing nor withdrawing his hand', shaping it for that purpose, until the eggs are hatched (p. 121).

So what are we to make of these stories? How are we to handle them? It is above all essential not to be romantic or sentimental. The creatures whom we meet in these pages are often at war with one another. They live lives of 'unbridled greed' (p. 73). They are delinquent. They betray kindliness with ingratitude. There is no attempt to deny their savagery and ferocity (p. 46). Nor is it ever forgotten that they naturally devour each other, just as it is entirely natural that the humans regularly catch and eat fish. So while there is much to say about the goodness of creation and the fine and fulfilling friendships between men and women and birds and animals, yet there is no denial of the darkness and brutality and cruelty which lies there also.

It is fascinating to find how much men and women have needed to have a sense of their relatedness to the animals. Although there is no mention of them in the gospels, from the very earliest times representations of the nativity have always included an ox and an ass standing by the manger, as if at the birth of Christ it was necessary for them to be beside the child. Speaking of one of the fifteenth-century icons of the Novgorod school, Ouspensky says that their place in the very centre of the scene points to the importance given by the Church to this detail.[1] This is nothing less than the fulfilment of the prophecy of Isaiah which has the deepest instructive

[1]*The Meaning of Icons*, Leonid Ouspensky and Vladimir Lossky, St Vladimir's Seminary Press (Crestwood, NY, 1989), pp. 157–9.

significance: 'The ox knows his owner, and the ass his master's crib.' According to the words of St. Gregory the Theologian, the nativity of Christ 'is not a festival of creation but a festival of re-creation': it is a renewal which sanctifies the whole world. Through the incarnation the whole of creation acquires a new meaning. So all creation is involved and takes part in the event. We see representatives of the whole created world, with angels, simple shepherds, the learned wise men, and not least the animals, each playing their role, each rendering their service, each giving thanks in their own way.

Since Helen Waddell first translated and made these stories available more than half a century ago, I feel, an extraordinary change has come over the consciousness of our thinking and we are now perhaps in a better position to appreciate and understand them than when this book was first published. There are both a new concern for the created world and a new way of looking at it. The destruction of the environment, the exploitation of natural resources, the despoiling of the earth and of many of its species have been brought vividly to our awareness, not necessarily by the Church, but more frequently by the ecologists and environmentalists and members of the green movement. The growth of science has brought about a very considerable shift in the way in which we are now beginning to look at the world, and to see the relationship of time and space and matter. Both this new concern and this new outlook converge here in these stories. The relationship of men and women with the earth and the natural creatures, and their shared, mutual dependency, is the very starting-point on which they depend. With the end of the purely rational and dualistic understanding of the world, of Newtonian physics and its logical categories and divisions, we are now beginning to speak in the terms of inter-connectedness, of the web of creation, of the network which brings all things together into a shared unity.

As we read them we are taken into the timeless world of story-telling: truth perceived by way of the imagination. They belong to the world in which truths about God and the world are expressed in story, legend, poetry; in which story-telling is a vehicle for religious understanding. We have for far too long been predominantly cerebral and rational, and only now are those nice neat categories which made everything so manageable being challenged. The holistic and imaginative approach that they call for in the reader may well come more naturally to us now as we begin to leave the mechanistic paradigms and move towards a more holistic approach to the world.[2]

These stories come from the Egyptian Desert Fathers and the Celtic saints. They come therefore from two traditions which are closely linked historically and spiritually. The connection of the two is visually represented by the dominating presence of the figures of St. Antony of Egypt and St. Paul of Thebes on so many of the Irish high crosses. For Celtic Christianity arrived in the Celtic countries which lay along the western sea coasts of the fringes of Europe, above all Ireland and Wales, by way of sea routes from the Eastern Mediterranean. It had from the first a monastic character with a strong eremetical emphasis, and it came from the desert to a deeply rural people who lived close to the earth, and whose religious beliefs were naturally shaped by their feeling for creation and the whole of the created world.

Here, in these early years – for the Desert Fathers belong to the fourth century and the Celtic saints to the sixth and seventh centuries (note, however, that there are in addition St. Werburga who died c.700 and St. Godric who died in 1170) – we are taken back to a holistic spirituality. Here is a profoundly significant return to our roots. For we are taken back beyond the Reformation and beyond the schism of East and West to those centuries that came out of the whole, orthodox, total tradition of the Church. I believe that this also

---

[2]The best clear and simple introduction to this is to be found in Diarmuid O'Murchu, *Our World in Transition*, Temple House Books (Sussex, 1992).

takes us back into what is early, primal and universal within
each one of us. The dualities which brought about the split
between matter and spirit, the material and the spiritual,
which have so shaped Christian faith and understanding in
recent centuries, hold no purchase here. Here too we find no
split between intellect and feelings, between the head and the
heart. The rediscovery of the Greek philosophers in the growth
of the universities in the twelfth century and the increasingly
general use of rational analysis shaped the education of succeeding centuries to the detriment of the imagination, the
feelings, the visual, the instinctive. If we are to recover something of the wholeness of the Christian tradition, and of our
own inner wholeness, then I believe it is to these early, creative
years that we should turn. And then, from that place, I also
believe that we shall be able to reach out to others, on the
fringes of the Churches, outside the Christian tradition, and
find that we can hear one another, and that what we say
carries common and shared resonances. Bede Griffiths hoped
that this new consciousness would provide a platform on
which religions would meet. 'We are beginning to discover
the unitive consciousness which goes beyond dualistic awareness', he said when he was awarded the John Herriott Mem-
orial prize in 1992.[3]

The experience of the men and women who appear in these
pages is of a religious universe, a dynamic universe: living,
powerful, a reflection of the power which comes from its
creator and maker. Men and women establish a relationship
with this universe, speaking to it, listening to it, trying to
create a harmony between it and themselves – for they are at
its centre, but they are not there to dominate, to control, to
organise. There is order, certainly, but it is the order of the
dance, not of the clock. Men and women are part of this order
as partners in a dance, not as observers of the skilful operation
of a celestial watchmaker. The creation in which we find

[3]*The Tablet*, 3 January 1993.

ourselves is not like being part of a machine: rather it is like being part of a continuing process in which God himself is still involved, constantly maintaining, empowering, renewing. For surely the men and women are also involved? After all, in Genesis 2, in the second creation story, God brings all the wild animals and the birds of heaven to man 'to see what he would call them'. Surely God might have known that himself? But perhaps he wished the human beings to have a part to play in the total canvas that he was painting, and in this naming the 'adam', the earthling, displays the kingly gift of wisdom in naming them, by which he both defines their natures and establishes authority over them. But does this mean to subdue and have dominion? After the flood comes the covenant in which God promises to care for both orders of creation, human and animal, and as Robert Murray says, 'One can only regret that no further implications for the mutual relations of human and animals are drawn out. Yet surely it is implicit that God is seen as promising to care for both orders of creatures, and if both are God's covenant partners how can they not be in some sense covenantually bound to each other?'[4]

That is the promise in the poem of Isaiah, that vision of peace and harmony between humans and animals. The humans are children, a young boy, a weaned child. Perhaps Adam and Eve were not created as adults but as children? Irenaeus and several other Church Fathers saw the innocence of the first man and woman as that of children (Murray, p. 109). Such scholarly debate is not appropriate here. But perhaps it is important for us to recognise the mutual enjoyment of the encounter of humans and animals in childlike innocence, the gentleness, and above all the playfulness. St. Columbanus walking in the woods to fast or to pray would call out to the creatures and they would come to him and he

[4]Robert Murray, *The Cosmic Covenant, Biblical Themes of Justice, Peace and the Integrity of Creation*, Sheed & Ward (London, 1992), p. 102.

would stroke and caress them 'and the wild things and the
birds would leap and frisk about him for sheer happiness,
jumping up on him as young dogs jump on their masters',
and he would have squirrels racing in and out of the folds of
his habit (p. 48). We can stay at this level or we can try to
see beyond it, as Sr Benedicta Ward helps us to do when she
interprets for us one of the most delightful of all these stories
(see pp. 55–7). St. Cuthbert has been praying at night in the
icy waters of the North Sea, and then two otters come and
lick his feet, wiping them with their skins and warming them
with their breath. To understand this aright she tells us we
must do as Bede did, and place over it the lens of the Scriptures. That hidden observer, the brother who is spying on him
in this hour of his most secret prayer, is not seeing a man
alone by the sea with two small furry animals rubbing round
his ankles, he is watching the epiphany of God by water and
by light, a moment of vision: 'He had not been watching a
man on a beach with his pets: he had seen the face of Christ
in a man so transfigured in prayer that the right order of
creation was in him restored. For Bede, St. Cuthbert . . . . was
the New Adam, once more at peace with all creation,
naming the animals, who were the first servant and the first
friend.'[5]

The saints whom we meet in these pages are for the most
part hermits, men and women who choose the life of solitude
because it fulfils a deep need and longing that they have for
silence and time apart to be alone with God. St. Cuthbert
leaves the demands of the monastery of Lindisfarne and sets
out 'in deep delight towards that secret solitude for which he
had so long desired and sought and striven. The coming and
going of the active life had done its long work upon him,
and he rejoiced that now he had earned his right to climb to
the quiet of meditation upon God' (p. 58).

[5]Sr Benedicta Ward SLG, *The Spirituality of St Cuthbert* (Fairacres, 1992),
p. 10.

'Steady in simplicity.' That is a marvellously simple phrase which catches something of the inner stillness which the hermit brings to these loving relationships with the creatures. It is used of St. Macarius of Alexandria when the hyena brings her sick whelp and holds it out to the old man, weeping, and he takes it from her and holds it in his hands 'steady in simplicity' (p. 12). The places to which they withdraw are deserts – the *dysart* or *disserth* of the Celtic lands, places apart which offer solitude and silence, and which come as a result to carry that same quality of stillness. So birds are drawn to the island of Farne because they have learned such gracious gentleness 'from the holiness of the place, or rather from those who made the place holy by their way of living there' (pp. 84–5).

When we read about their lives, and see how often the wild creatures become part of them (even to the extent of being described as fellow monks or disciples), we find ourselves taken into that mysterious co-inherence which links the creator with mankind and with the creatures. Here is a very powerful starting-point to the idea of common creation. The hermit who seems to leave the world and might appear to be shunning or escaping it is in fact simply living from a centre which unites him or her with the whole unity of being.

These stories will probably speak to many people at the point at which they are most poignantly aware of a need to encounter the solitary self, the secret and innermost hermit of their own selves. Many ordinary lay people are today increasingly finding how much they need that solitude, and how much it brings them an awareness not only of their own selves in relation to God but also their relationship with the world as well. 'The very nature of your solitude involves you in union with the prayers of the wind in the trees, the movement of the stars, the feeding of the birds in the fields, the building of the anthills. You witness the creator and attend to him in all his creation.' These are the words of John Howard Griffin, friend of Thomas Merton, as he lived at intervals in

INTRODUCTION

Merton's hermitage and there discovered in twentieth-century
terms something which is ageless, and which united him with
these hermits of fifteen hundred years before. He goes on to
say, 'This is not for one moment mere pantheism. You do not
"worship" the thing, but the creator of the thing. The thing
fascinates precisely because it raises your attention through
its beauty or interest above itself to the creator . . .'[6]

'Understand creation and you will then understand the
creator' is one of the great cries of the Celtic saints. The way
in which they saw the world, and came to love and to know
it, was above all because they lived out of a contemplative
centre. What shaped their vision was a life of contemplative
prayer. Merton once spoke of creation being given to men and
women 'as a clear window through which the light of God
would shine into men's souls. All created things are trans-
parent. They speak to men not of themselves but of the God
who made them.'

In these stories we are able to move easily between two
worlds, the known and the natural world of present reality
and the world of the unknown and the supernatural beyond
the present. We are given vignettes, like strong shafts or beams
which in one piercing moment illuminate for us those total
lives of prayer-filled dedication to God which otherwise we
might never glimpse. These are no more than moments, events
or happenings given to us for their significance in the relationship of these men and women to God, caught for us, in lives
which were being gradually entirely filled, transfigured with
the presence of God in Christ reconciling the world to himself.[7]

These lives are shown to us for the inspiration which they
bring to us who are also trying to make our way in the world
of God's creating, and to travel along the path of our own
Christian discipleship. We all, being human, need the help

[6]John Howard Griffin, *The Hermitage Journals. Diary kept while Working
on the Biography of Thomas Merton*, Conger Beasley Jr (ed.), Andrews and
McNeel Inc. (Kansas City, MO, 1981), p. 14.
[7]Ward, op. cit., p. 13.

[xxvii]

and encouragement of holy people. The legends of saints will endure since they serve this deep need that we have: to believe that what we long for is possible. Here are men and women who, because they have first found God in themselves, can then encounter him in the world outside themselves. Here are lives in which miracle is commonplace and in which the world of present reality is absorbed into an all-encompassing, all-pervading supernatural world, one above all which speaks to us of that harmony and unity of the whole of creation for which we all so deeply long.[8]

NOTE ON ROBERT GIBBINGS

'Engravings are as much a part of *book making* as of *illustration*. They don't merely illustrate the text, they also decorate the book.' This, which Eric Gill wrote when in the 1920s he was working closely with Robert Gibbings, is a nice comment on why it seemed important to me in this new edition to keep Robert Gibbings' original wood-engravings. He was an extremely keen observer of natural life and made detailed sketches of birds and animals which he would translate into wood-engravings. These were always engraved with exceptional cleanness of outline. His simple masses of black and white have an extra solidity given to them by the cross-hatching work with the graver which merges the black into the white with the grey. They are very much an integral part of the whole, bringing together the written and the visual, the human and the creatures, which is part of the essential charm, and the importance, of this small book.

[8] I owe this last phrase to William Marnell, *Light from the West, The Irish Mission and the Emergence of Modern Europe*, Seabury Press (New York, 1978).

THE DESERT FATHERS

THE HERMIT'S GARDEN IN THE DESERT

WHEN I first entered the desert, about twelve miles from the Nile – I had one of the brethen for guide, a man who knew the country well – we came to where an old monk lived at the foot of a mountain. And there, a thing very rare in those parts, was a well. He had an ox, whose sole business it was to draw up the water by turning a wheel: for the well was said to be a thousand or more feet deep. He had a garden too,

[3]

full of many sorts of vegetables: a thing against
nature in the desert, where everything is so parched
and burnt by the rays of the sun that it seldom
gives root or seed, and then but scant. But the
labour that the saint shared with his ox, and his
own industry, were to profit: for the constant water-
ing gave such richness to the sand that we saw the
herbs growing in the garden, green and lavish. On
these the ox lived, together with his master: and
from this plenty the good man provided a feast for
us as well. I saw then what you men of Gaul will
hardly believe, the pot of vegetables that he was
preparing for our meal boiling without any fire
under it: so great is the heat of the sun that it would
cook a Gallic meal as well as any cooks you please.

After supper, as evening drew on, he invited us
to a palm tree, the fruit of which he sometimes
used; it was about two miles away. For these trees
indeed exist in the desert, though not many: and
whether it was the skill of the men of old time, or
the nature of the soil, begat them, I know not:
or else God foreseeing that the desert would some
day be inhabited by the saints, prepared them for
His servants. For the most part, those who live in
these remote solitudes live on the fruit of these trees,
since no other succeeds in growing here.

We came then to this tree, led by our kindly host:
and there stumbled upon a lion. At sight of him,
my guide and I quaked, but the saintly old man
went unfalteringly on, and we followed him, timor-

[4]

ously enough. The wild beast – you would say it was at the command of God – modestly withdrew a little way and sat down, while the old man plucked the fruit from the lower branches. He held out his hand, full of dates; and up the creature ran and took them as frankly as any tame animal about the house: and when it had finished eating, it went away. We stood, watching and trembling; reflecting, as well we might, what valour of faith was in him, and what poverty of spirit in us.

THE PENITENT WOLF

ANOTHER man, no less remarkable, we saw, living in a poor hut, where only one could enter at a time. The story was told of him that a she-wolf used to stand beside him at his meal, and that never did the creature fail to come at the appointed time, or to wait outside until he offered her whatever bread had been left over from his poor meal: and then she would lick his hand, and as if her task were over and the comfort of her presence duly given, would go away.

But it once so happened that the holy man had gone with a brother who had come to see him, to put him on his way, and was a long time absent, not getting home until nightfall. Meantime the beast had come at the usual meal hour. She felt that her friend and patron was absent, and went into his empty cell, inquisitive to find where its inhabitant might be. By chance a palm-basket with five loaves was hanging within reach: she ventured to take one, devoured it, and then, the crime perpetrated, made off.

The hermit came in, and saw his basket torn: he perceived the damage his household store had suffered, and near the threshold he recognized the crumbs where someone had been eating bread: nor had he much doubt as to the person of the thief. Then as the days went by and the creature did not come – too conscious of her bold act to come to him she had wronged, and affect innocence – the hermit took it sorely to heart that he had lost the company of his pet. At last when the seventh day had gone by, his prayers were answered: there she was, as he sat at his meal, as of old. But it was easy to perceive the embarrassment of the penitent: she stood, not daring to come near, her eyes fixed in profound shame upon the ground, and plainly entreating pardon. Pitying her confusion, the hermit called her to come near, and with a caressing hand he stroked the sad head: and finally, refreshed his penitent with two loaves for one. And she, forgiveness won and her grieving ended, resumed her wonted office. Consider, I pray you, in this example of it the power of Christ, with whom every brute beast is wise, and every savage creature gentle.

THE BLESSED AMMON AND
THE DRAGONS

SO then, we had taken leave of the blessed Apollonius and were journeying to the parts of the desert over against the south, when we saw in the sand the marks of the trail of a huge dragon: it was as if a beam had been dragged over the sand, so vast did it appear to be. At the sight of it, we were terror-stricken. But the brethren who were our guides exhorted us to be in no fear whatever, but rather to have faith and follow the dragon's tracks. 'For you shall see,' said they, 'what faith can do, when you behold him extinguished by us. Many a dragon and serpent and horned beast have we slain with our hands, even as it is written that the Lord gave them that believed in Him power to tread upon serpents and scorpions and over all the power of the enemy.' But even as they spoke, the frailty of our unbelief made us quake more and more, and we begged them not to follow the tracks of the dragon, but keep to our own straight course. One of them, however, in the keenness of his spirit, would himself go after the dragon: and finding her cave not far off, shouted at us to come over to him, and we should see what befell.

At this point, however, a brother who lived in the desert close by, came up to us and forbade us to follow the dragon, declaring that we could not endure the sight of her, especially as we were not in the habit of seeing the like: he said that he himself had often seen this very beast: that she was of incredible bulk, and fifteen cubits in length. And after urging us to go to his own house, he himself hurried off to bring away the brother, who was standing waiting for us yonder, all in trim for the slaying of the beast, and made him come back with him, reluctant as he was to leave without destroying her: he had much ado to turn him from his purpose. And when he had come up with us, he had many hard words for our poor-spiritedness and lack of faith.

So, arrived at our friend's cell, we sat down to rest, and had no small kindness from him. He told us that in this place where he himself was living, there had dwelt a holy man whose disciple he himself had been: his name was Ammon; and the Lord had done mighty wonders through him. And among others, he told us this tale.

Often, he said, thieves would come to him and steal his bread, which was all he lived on, and whatever of his meagre store he might have laid aside. Again and again he suffered this molestation from them: till one day he set out into the desert and led home with him two enormous dragons to be in attendance on him, instructing them to stay by his monastery gate, and guard the entrance. Up came the thieves as usual, not knowing what custodians were now posted at the threshold: and at sight of

[9]

the dragons, their wits and their strength went from them, and they fell speechless to the ground. And when the old man was aware, he came out, found them half dead, and picking them up, scolded them, saying, 'See now how much hardier you be than the beasts: for these obey me for God's sake, whereas ye not only have no fear of God, but think it no shame to harry His servants.' Nevertheless he brought them into his cell, set a table before them and bade them eat. And they, touched to the heart and all their inhumanity abandoned, in a short while became better men than many who had begun to serve God long before them. . . .

Another time it befell that a most brutal dragon was laying waste the countryside and slaughtering many: and the country folk came to this Father, begging him to rid the place of this beast. At the same time, to rouse the old man's pity, they carried with them a lad, a shepherd's son, who had been struck to the ground in terror at the mere sight of the dragon, and was left lifeless and swollen from the creature's breath. He anointed the lad with oil, and made him well again. But meantime, although inwardly he was spurring himself to the slaying of the dragon, he would promise them nothing, making as though he could be of no help to them.

Next morning he was up early, and on his way to the dragon's retreat: and there, setting his knees upon the ground, he entreated the Lord. Then the beast with a mighty rush came out upon him, breathing black foul fumes and uttering hisses and shrill shrieks. But he, in no way perturbed, turned towards the dragon and said, 'May Christ the Son of God slay thee, even as He shall slay the great whale.' And at the old man's word, that most dire dragon vomited forth its spirit and its venom together, and burst asunder with a loud crack. And all the dwellers in that countryside came up and stood dumb at so mighty a miracle: and unable to bear the vehement stench, they heaped on him vast mounds of sand, while Father Ammon still stood by: for even though the creature were dead, they dared not come near it unless he were by.

ST. MACARIUS OF ALEXANDRIA AND
THE GRATEFUL HYÆNA

IT happened one day as he was sitting in his cell, a hyæna came to him, her whelp was in her mouth; she set it down beside the door, she knocked on the door with her head. The old man heard her knock, he came out thinking that a brother had come to him. When he opened the door he saw the hyæna, he was astounded, saying, 'What does she want here?' She filled her mouth with her whelp, she held it out to the old man, weeping. The old man took the whelp in his hands, steady in simplicity, he turned it this way and that, looking in its body for what ailed it. When he had considered the whelp, behold, it was blind in its two eyes. He took it, he groaned, he spat on its face, he signed it on the eyes with his finger: straightway the whelp saw, it went to its mother's dug, it sucked, it followed her, they went away to that river ... and into the marsh they made their way. The sheep of the Lybians, they bring them once each year into the marsh of Scete to eat the *shoushet*, and the herdsmen that live in the villages over against Pernouj, they also bring their oxen into the marsh of Scete to eat the green herbage, once a year.

The hyæna left a day behind her. The next day she came to the old man, she had a sheepskin in her mouth, thick with wool, freshly killed, she had it over her; she struck the door with her head. The old man was sitting in the enclosure. When he heard the knock at the door, he got up, he opened it: he found the hyæna, the sheepskin over her. He said to the hyæna, 'Where hast thou been? Where hast thou found this, if thou hast not eaten a sheep? As that which thou has brought me comes of violence, I will not take it.'

The hyæna struck her head upon the ground, she bent her paws, and on her knees she prayed him, as if she had been a man, to take it. He said to her, 'I have but now told thee that I will not take it, unless thou makest me this promise: *I will not vex the poor by eating their sheep.*' She made many movements of her head, up and down, as if she were promising him. Again he repeated it to her, saying, 'Unless thou dost promise me, saying, *I will not kill a creature alive*; but from to-day thou wilt eat thy prey when it is dead. If thou art distressed, seeking and finding none, come hither, and I will give thee bread. From this hour, do hurt to no creature.' And the hyæna bowed her head to the ground, and dropped on her knees, bending her paws, moving her head up and down, looking at his face as if she were promising him. And the old man perceived in his heart that it was the purpose of God who gives understanding to beasts for a reproach unto ourselves, and he gave glory to God who gives understanding to the beasts, he sang in the Egyptian tongue God who liveth for ever, for the soul hath honour: he said, 'I give glory to Thee, O God, who wast with Daniel in the lion's den, who didst give understanding unto beasts: also Thou hast given understanding to this hyæna and Thou hast not forgotten me: but Thou hast made me perceive, that it is Thy ordering. And the old man took the skin from the hyæna, and she went away. From time to time she would come to seek the old man; if she had not been able to find food, she would come to him and he would throw her a loaf. She did this many a time. And the old man slept on the skin until he died. And I have seen it with my own eyes.

ST. PACHOME, ABBOT OF TABENNE, AND THE CROCODILES

AT another time the cohorts of the devils plotted to tempt the man of God by a certain phantasy. For a crowd of them assembling together, were seen by him tying up the leaf of a tree with great ropes and tugging it along with immense exertion, ranked in order on the right and the left: and the one side would exhort the other, and strain and tug, as if they were moving a stone of enormous weight. And this the wicked spirits were doing so as to move him, if they could, to loud laughter, and so they might cast it in his teeth. But Pachome, seeing their impudence, groaned, and fled to the Lord with his accustomed prayers: and straightway by the virtue of Christ all their triangular array was brought to naught. . . .

After this, so much trust had the blessed Pachome learned to place in God . . . that many a time he trod on snakes and scorpions, and passed unhurt through all: and the crocodiles, if ever he had necessity to cross the river, would carry him with the utmost subservience, and set him down at whatever spot he indicated.

THE ABBOT HELENUS AND
THE WILD ASS

AT one time he was on his way to visit certain brethren who were ill, and carrying with him such things as the comfort of their bodies required. But as he walked, the heavy load that he carried began to distress him; and seeing some distance off a herd of wild asses crossing the desert, he cried out to them, saying, 'In the name of our Lord Jesus Christ, let one of you come here and take my pack.' And lo, one out of the whole herd made its way to him, in all gentleness. And so he set his load on the willing creature, and himself as well, and was carried with all swiftness to the cells of the brethren whither he was journeying.

THE ABBOT HELENUS AND
THE CROCODILE

HE came at one time upon certain monks, upon a Sabbath day, and said them, 'Why are ye not at Mass?' They made plain reply, 'Because the priest has not come.' Then said he, 'I shall go and call him.' Then they said that no one could cross the river, because of the depth of its channel. Also they said that there was a great beast in that place, namely a crocodile, who had eaten many men.

He, nevertheless, made no tarrying, but straightway getting up, made his way to the ford: and the crocodile at once took him upon its back and ferried him over to the opposite bank. He found the priest in the fields, and prayed him not to neglect the brotherhood. The priest, seeing him hung about with many patched rags, asked him where he got his coat, saying, 'Thou hast a most fair garment for thy soul, my brother,' and marvelling at his humility and frugality, followed him on his way to the river. And when they could find no skiff to ferry them across, the Abbot Helenus sent out a shout, to summon the crocodile. She at once obediently came up, and flattened her back: the Abbot invited the priest to mount along with him: but he, stricken with alarm at sight of the crocodile, retraced his steps. And great was his admiration, and that of the brethren on the further bank, when they saw the Abbot crossing the river upon a crocodile. Climbing up the bank, he drew the crocodile after him, saying, 'Better is it for her that she should die, than suffer the penalty for the slaughter of souls.' And the crocodile fell down, and died on the spot.

ST. SIMEON STYLITES AND THE
CONVERTED DRAGON

THE fame of the holy man increased throughout the world, and they built him a pillar twelve cubits high, and he stood upon it twelve years. And again they built him a pillar twenty cubits high, and he stood upon it twelve years. Then all that dwelt in that place came together, and they built two churches beside the pillar, and a pillar thirty cubits high, and he stood upon it four years, and began to do miracles. . . . And many people he turned to the Christian faith, namely Saracens and Persians and Armenians and Laotians and the Foreigners. . . .

And after these days they again built him a pillar forty cubits high, and he stood upon it for sixteen years until his death. Now at that time there was an exceeding large dragon that lived close by, in the country to the north: and because of him no grass ever grew there: and a branch of a tree fell into his right eye. And lo, one day the blind dragon came, dragging himself along, and he applied himself to the pillar which was the habitation of the man of God, and winding himself into a wheel as if to ask pardon, lay with his head bowed low. And the blessed Simeon gazed down upon him and straightway, the branch fell out of his eye: and it was a cubit in length. And indeed all that saw it glorified God, notwithstanding that they fled from him in terror. But the creature coiled itself up and stayed quiet in one place, whilst all the people went by. Then rising up, it worshipped at the gate of the monastery for wellnigh two hours, and so returned to its den, and did no hurt to any.

THE UNSOCIABLE LION

THERE was a certain old man, a solitary, who lived near the river of Jordan: and going into a cave because of the heat, he found there a lion: and the lion began to gnash his teeth, and to roar. To whom the old man said, 'What is annoying thee? There is room enough here to hold both me and thee. And if thou likest it not, arise and go hence.' But the lion, not taking it well, left and went outside.

THE ABBOT GERASIMUS AND THE LION

ABOUT a mile distant from the Jordan is a monastery, called after the Abbot Gerasimus. On our coming to the monastery the old men who dwelt there told us of the Abbot Gerasimus, how one day walking on the banks of the Jordan he met a lion making a mighty roaring, and one paw dangling: and sticking in the paw was the sharp point of a reed, so that the paw was swollen and full of matter. When the lion saw the old man, it showed him the paw with the thorn fixed in it, weeping after its fashion and beseeching him to have some care of it. And the old man seeing him in such sore straits, sat down and took the paw, opened it and drew out the thorn with a great deal of pus, cleansed the wound carefully, bound it up with a rag, and sent him away. But the lion finding himself cured would not leave the old man, but followed after him wherever he went as a dear disciple his master, so that the old man marvelled at the gratitude of a wild beast. And thenceforward the old man would feed him, setting bread before him and soaked herbs.

Now the monastery had a donkey to draw water from the Jordan for the brethren's needs. And the old man made it a rule that the lion should take charge of the donkey. And so he would go off with him along the banks of the Jordan, and watch him

grazing. But one day while the donkey was brows-
ing the lion had gone some little distance away;
and lo! a camel driver from Arabia came upon the
donkey and took him and led him away. The lion,
his donkey lost, returned sorely dejected to the monastery, and came with drooping head and neck
before his abbot. Now the Abbot Gerasimus
thought that he had devoured the donkey, and said,
'Where is the donkey?' He stood silent and downcast, like any man. Then said the old man, 'Thou
hast eaten him: blessed be God. Whatsoever the ass
did, from this time forward thou shalt do.' After
which, at the old man's bidding, the lion wore pan-
niers that held four jars, and carried the water for
the monastery.

Now one day a certain soldier came to the old
man for his blessing, and when he saw the lion
carrying his burden and learned the reason, he was
sorry for him, and offered three pieces of money to
the old men to buy a donkey for this business of
water-carrying, and release the lion from that
necessity. A little while had gone by after his deliverance from this task, when the camel driver who
had stolen the donkey was coming with barley to
sell it in the Holy City, and the donkey with him.
He had crossed the Jordan where he came upon
the lion: and at the sight of him he left his camels
and fled. The lion, recognizing the donkey, ran up
to him, and holding the halter in his mouth as he
was wont, drew him along with the three camels,

and jubilant and roaring at finding his lost donkey, came to the old man. The old man who had originally thought that the lion had eaten the donkey now perceived that he had been taken unawares. And he called the lion Jordanes. And for more than five years the lion went about among the brethren in the monastery, never quitting the old man.

But when the Abbot Gerasimus passed over to the Lord, and was buried by the fathers, it befel, by the dispensation of God, that the lion was not to be found. After a little while he comes in, and begins looking for his old master. The Abbot Sabbatius Cilix, who had been disciple to the Abbot Gerasimus, saw him and said, 'Jordanes, our old master has left us orphans, and has passed over to the Lord: yet take and eat.' But the lion would not eat, but went ceaselessly here and there, turning about and looking round to see his old master, and signifying by a mighty roaring that he could not bear him to be absent. The Abbot Sabbatius and the other old men would ruffle his head and say to him, 'The old master has gone to God and left us.' But nothing they said could appease his roaring and lamenting: for the more they tried to caress and console him the more he grieved and the louder he roared, adding lament upon lament, and showing in voice and visage and eye the grief that he was in at not seeing the old man.

Then the Abbot Sabbatius said to him, 'Come with me, since you will not believe us, and I will show you where our old master is laid.' and he took him and led him to where they had buried him. It was about five paces from the church. And the Abbot Sabbatius, standing by the grave of the Abbot Gerasimus, said to the lion, 'Look: our old master is buried here.' And the Abbot Sabbatius bowed his knees beside the old man's grave. And when the lion heard it and saw the Abbot Sabbatius prone upon the grave and weeping, he laid himself down, beating his head upon the earth and roaring: and he died there, on the old man's grave.

ST. JEROME AND THE LION AND
THE DONKEY

IMPOSSIBLE and long it would be to unfold all that might be told of that great man and his austere life and ways. Yet one miracle about this monastery there is, like those of old time, that oblivion hath not yet stolen from memory, for it is handed down from one to another, and told by holy men that lived in Bethlehem for love of the heavenly fatherland: and it I now weave into this compendious discourse.

Upon a certain day as evening drew on, and the blessed Jerome sat with the brethren, as is the way of the monk, to hear the reading of the lesson and to speak good words, lo of a sudden, limping on three paws and the fourth caught up, came a mighty lion into the cloister. At sight of him a good many of the brethren fled in terror, for human frailty is but timorous. But the blessed Jerome went out to meet him as one greets an incoming guest.

And while the distance between them was shortening, the lion who had no way of speaking, it not being his nature, offered the good father as best he might his wounded paw: and the Saint, calling the brethren, gave instructions that the wounded paw should be bathed, to find why the lion went thus limping. Upon close examination, they found that the paw had been pierced by thorns. Fomentations were applied with all diligence, and the wound speedily healed.

And now, all wildness and savagery laid aside, the lion began to go to and fro among them as peaceable and domestic as any animal about the house. This the blessed Jerome observed, and spoke as follows to the brethren: 'Bring your minds to bear upon this, my brethren: what, I ask you, can we find for this lion to do in the way of useful and suitable work, that will not be burdensome to him, and that he can efficiently accomplish? For I believe of a surety that it was not so much for the healing of his paw that God sent him hither, since He could have cured him without us, as to show us that He is anxious to provide marvellous well for our necessity.'

To which the brethren gave concerted and humble response: 'Thou knowest, father, that the donkey who brings us our wood from the forest pasture needs some one to look after him, and that we are always in fear that some naughty beast will devour him. Wherefore if it seem to thee good and right, let the charge of our donkey be laid upon the lion, that he may take him out to pasture, and again may bring him home.'

And so it was done: the donkey was put in charge of the lion, as his shepherd: together they took the road to the pasture, and wherever the donkey grazed, there was his defender: and a sure defence he was. Nevertheless, at regular hours, that he might refresh himself and the donkey do his appointed task, the lion would come with him home.

And so for long enough it was: till one day, the donkey duly brought to his pasture, the lion felt a great weight of sluggishness come upon him, and he fell asleep. And as he lay sunk in deep slumber, it befell that certain merchants came along that road on their way to Egypt to buy oil. They saw the donkey grazing, they saw that no guardian was at hand, and seized by sudden wicked greed, they caught him and led him away.

In due course the lion roused up, knowing nothing of his loss, and set out to fetch his charge at graze. But when he was not to be seen in the accustomed pasture, constricted with anxiety and in deep distress the lion went roaring up and down, hither and thither, for the remainder of the day, seeking what he had lost. And at last, when all hope of finding the donkey was gone, he came and stood at the monastery gate.

Conscious of guilt, he no longer dared walk in as of old time with his donkey. The blessed Jerome saw him, and the brethren too, hanging about outside the gate, without the donkey, and long past his usual hour: and they concluded that he had been tempted by hunger to kill his animal. In no mind, therefore, to offer him his wonted ration, 'Away with you,' said they, 'and finish up whatever you have left of the donkey, and fill your greedy belly.'

And yet even as they spoke, they were doubtful as to whether he had indeed perpetrated this crime or no.

So finally the brethren went out to the pasture whither the lion was wont to bring the animal afore-said, and up and down they scoured, to see if they could find any trace of the slaughter. No sign of violence was to be seen: and turning home they made haste to bring their report to the blessed Jerome. He heard them, and spoke. 'I entreat you, brethren,' said he, 'that although ye have suffered the loss of the ass, do not, nevertheless, nag at him or make him wretched. Treat him as before, and offer him his food: and let him take the donkey's place, and make a light harness for him so that he can drag home the branches that have fallen in the wood.' And it was done.

So the lion did regularly his appointed task, while the time drew on for the merchants to return. Then one day, his work done, he went out, inspired as I believe, brute beast though he was, by some divine prompting, and made his way to the field. Up and down, hither and thither in circles he ran, craving some further light on the fate that had befallen his comrade. And finally, worn out but still anxious, he climbed on to a rising above the highway where he might look all around him. A great way off he spied men coming with laden camels, and in front of them walked a donkey. So far off was he that he could not recognize him. None the less he set out, stepping cautiously, to meet them.

Now it is said to be the custom in that part of the country that whenever men set out with camels on a long journey, a donkey goes in front, with the camel's halter on its neck, and the camels follow after. And now the merchants came nearer, and he recognized his donkey. With a fierce roar he charged down upon them, making a mighty din, though doing no damage to any. Crazed with terror, as they well might be, they left all they had and took to their heels, the lion meantime roaring terribly and lashing the ground with his tail: and so he drove the affrighted camels, laden as they were, back to the monastery before him.

So when this surprising sight met the brethren's gaze, the donkey pacing in the van, the lion in like fashion marching in the rear, and the laden beasts in the middle, they slipped quietly away to inform the blessed Jerome. He came out, and benevolently bade them to set open the monastery gate, enjoining them to silence. 'Take their loads off these our guests,' said he, 'the camels, I mean, and the donkey, and bathe their feet and give them fodder, and wait to see what God is minded to show His servants.'

Then, when all instructions as to the camels had been obeyed, began the lion as of old to go here and there in high feather through the cloister, flattening himself at the feet of each several brother and wagging his tail, as though to ask forgiveness for the crime that he had never committed. Whereupon

the brethren, full of remorse for the cruel charge
they had brought against him, would say to one
another, 'Behold our trusty shepherd whom so short
a while ago we were upbraiding for a greedy ruf-
fian, and God has deigned to send him to us with
such a resounding miracle, to clear his character!'
Meantime the blessed Jerome, aware of things to
come, spoke to the brethren, saying, 'Be prepared,
my brethren, in all things that are requisite for
refreshment: so that those who are about to be
our guests may be received, as is fitting, without
embarrassment.'

His orders duly obeyed, and the brethren chatting
with the blessed Jerome, suddenly comes a messenger with the news that there are guests without the
gate, desirous to see the Father of the community.
At this, the already frequently named Father commanded that the doors of the monastery be opened,
and the visitors brought to him. They, however,
in spite of this invitation, came in blushing, and
prostrated themselves at the feet of the blessed
Jerome, entreating forgiveness for their fault.
Gently raising them up, he admonished them to
enjoy their own with thanksgiving, but not to
encroach on others' goods: and in short to live cautiously, as ever in the presence of God. And this
marvellous discourse ended, he bade them accept
refreshment, and take again their camels and go
their way.

Then with one voice they cried out, 'We entreat

you, Father, that you will accept, for the lamps in the church and the necessity of the brethren, half of the oil that the camels have brought: because we know and are sure that it was rather to be of service to you than for our own profit that we went down into Egypt to bargain there.' To which the blessed Jerome replied, 'This that you ask is indeed not right, for it would seem a great hardship that we who ought to have compassion on others and relieve their necessities by our own giving, should bear so heavy on you, taking your property away from you when we are not in need of it.'

To which they answer: 'Neither this food, nor any of our own property do we touch, unless you first command that what we ask shall be done. And so, as we have said, do you now accept half of the oil that the camels have brought: and we pledge ourselves and our heirs to give to you and those that come after you the measure of oil which is called a hin in each succeeding year.'

So therefore, constrained and compelled by the violence of their entreaties, the blessed Jerome commanded that their prayer should be fulfilled. They partook of refreshment, and after receiving both benediction and camels, they returned exultant and jocund to their own people. But that these things were done at Bethlehem, and the fashion of their doing, is confidently related among the inhabitants of that place until this day.

THE SAINTS OF THE WEST

THE DEATH OF KING TEUDIRIC

KING Teudiric had kept peace and justice with his people for the years that he held kingship, till such time as he laid aside the temporal power for ever, in that he commended his kingdom to his son Mouric, and began to live a hermit life in the cliffs of Tintern. But while he was in that life, the Saxons began to invade his land against Mouric his son, and beyond himself there was none to help, that his son might not be driven from his inheritance by strangers. Of Teudiric it was said in the days when he held his kingdom that never had he been vanquished by the enemy but ever was the victor, and that once his face was seen in the battle-line straightway the enemy were driven to flight. And the night before, the angel of the Lord said to him: 'To-morrow go to the help of the people of God against the enemies of the Church of Christ, and the foe shall turn their face in flight as far as Brockwere, and do thou stand armed in the battle-line, and when thy face as in time past is seen and known, they shall take to flight. And hereafter for XXX years they shall not dare to come against thy country in thy son's time, and the men of thy land and their sons that come after them shall be in quiet peace: and thou thyself shalt be wounded with a thrust above Tintern, and after three days thou shalt die in peace.'

So in the morning he rose as the army of Mouric, his son, came by, and he mounted his horse and rode with them joyous of the bidding of the angel. And he stood in armour in the battle-line above the bank of the Wye near Tintern ford. And at the sight of his face they turned their backs and fled, yet one of them hurled a lance and the lance wounded him even as he had been told, and he rejoiced over it, as a man rejoices over the rout of his foe and the taking of the spoil. Then Mouric, his son, returning victorious with the captured spoil, would have his father come with him. And he said, 'I will not go from this place until my Lord Jesus Christ shall bear me hence to the place of my desire, to the island of Echni, where I have willed to lie after my death.'

And in the morning at dawn there were two stags yoked and ready with his bier before his lodging. And the man of God, knowing that they were sent on God's behalf, ascended the bier; and wherever they rested, there springs welled up, until they came to a place beside a meadow towards the Severn Sea. And after they had come to that place, a spring of clearest water welled up and swept the bier asunder, and straightway he commended his soul to God and bade the stags depart: and there he remained alone, and after a while gave up the ghost.

ST. COLUMBA AND THE CRANE

AND another time it befell, while the Saint was living on Iona, that he called one of the brethren to him, to speak to him. 'Go thou,' he said, 'three days from now to the west of this island at dawn, and sit above the shore and wait: for when the third hour before sunset is past, there shall come flying from the northern coast of Ireland a stranger guest, a crane, wind tossed and driven far from her course in the high air: tired out and weary she will fall on the beach at thy feet and lie there, her strength nigh gone: tenderly lift her and carry her to the steading near by: make her welcome there and cherish her with all care for three days and nights; and when the three days are ended, refreshed and loath to tarry longer with us in our exile, she shall take flight again towards that old sweet land of Ireland whence she came, in pride of strength once more: and if I commend her so earnestly to thy charge, it is that in that countryside where thou and I were reared, she too was nested.'

The brother obeyed: and on the third day, when the third hour before sunset was past, stood as he was bidden, in wait for the coming of the promised guest: and when she had come and lay fallen on the beach, he lifted her and carried her ailing to the steading, and fed her, famished as she was. And on his return that evening to the monastery the Saint spoke to him, not as one questioning but as one speaks of a thing past. 'May God bless thee, my son,' said he, 'for thy kind tending of this pilgrim guest: that shall make no long stay in her exile, but when three suns have set shall turn back to her own land.'

And the thing fell out even as the Saint had foretold. For when her three days housing was ended, and as her host stood by, she rose in first flight from the earth into high heaven, and after a while at gaze to spy out her aerial way, took her straight flight above the quiet sea, and so to Ireland through the tranquil weather.

ST. COLUMBA AND THE WHITE HORSE

O N a day in the month of May, the old man
set out to visit the brethren at their work:
and weary with the years that were upon
him, he made the journey in a cart. He found them
busy in the western fields of the island: and that
day he spoke to them. 'I had a great longing on
me,' he said, 'this April just now past, in the high
days of the Easter feast, to go to the Lord Christ:

and it was granted me by Him, if I so willed. But I would not have the joy of your feast turned into mourning, and so I willed to put off the day of my going from the world a little longer.' But at this heavy saying his monks were sorely downcast, and he began to hearten them as well as he might. And that done, sitting as he was in the cart, and turning his face to the east, he blessed the island and the islanders that dwelt upon it; and from that day, as is written in the book I have already spoken of, the poison in the triple-forked tongue of the viper has done no hurt to man or to beast, until this day. And so he uttered the words of his blessing, and was carried back to his monastery. . . .

At the end of that same week, that is on the Saturday, the venerable old man and his faithful Diarmid who tended him set out to the blessing of a barn near by. And going inside, the Saint blessed it, and two heaps of grain that were stored there: and then with a gesture of thanksgiving, he spoke, 'Truly,' said he, 'I give my brethren at home joy that this year, if so be I might have to go somewhere away from you, you will have what provision will last you the year.'

But at that, Diarmid his man began to grieve and said, 'You have saddened us too often this year, my father, with this talk of yours about going away.' And the Saint made answer, 'I have a small secret word to say to you; and if you would give me your promise to reveal it to no one before my death, I

could tell you more openly abut my going.' And
when the asked for promise had been given, his
man kneeling before him, the saintly old man spoke.
'In the Holy Book,' he said, 'this day is called the
Sabbath, which is, being interpreted, rest. And truly
is this day my Sabbath, for it is the last day for me
of this present toilsome life, when from all weariness of travail I shall take my rest, and at midnight
of this Lord's Day that draws on, I shall as the
Scripture saith, go the way of my fathers. For now
my Lord Jesus Christ hath deigned to invite me;
and to Him, I say, at this very midnight and at His
own desiring, I shall go. For so it was revealed to
me by the Lord himself.' At this sad hearing his
man began bitterly to weep, and the Saint tried to
comfort him as best he might.

And so the Saint left the barn, and took the road
back to the monastery: and halfway there sat down
to rest. Afterwards on that spot they set a cross,
planted upon a millstone, and it is to be seen by
the roadside to this day. And as the Saint sat there,
a tired old man taking his rest awhile, up runs the
white horse, his faithful servitor that used to carry
the milk pails, and coming up to the Saint he leaned
his head against his breast and began to mourn,
knowing as I believe from God Himself – for to
God every animal is wise in the instinct his Maker
hath given him – that his master was soon to go
from him, and that he would see his face no more:
and his tears ran down as a man's might into the

[44]

lap of the Saint, and he foamed as he wept. Seeing it, Diarmid would have driven the sorrowing creature away, but the Saint prevented him saying, 'Let be, let be, suffer this lover of mine to shed on my breast the tears of his most bitter weeping. Behold, you that are a man and have a reasonable soul could in no way have known of my departing if I had not but now told you: yet to this dumb and irrational beast, his Creator in such fashion as pleased Him has revealed that his master is to go from him.' And so saying, he blessed the sad horse that had served him, and it turned again to its way.

ST. COLUMBAN IN THE VOSGES

IT was in these parts it befell that while the saint was walking in the dark woods, a book on his shoulder, and arguing with himself about Holy Writ, the thought came suddenly to his mind whether he would rather choose to suffer the outrage of men, or the savagery of beasts. His thought drove him hard, and he would often cross himself and pray: and finally he said to himself that it was better to suffer the ferocity of wild beasts that was no sin of theirs, than the cruelty of men, to the loss of their own souls. And even as he turned this over in his mind, he saw twelve wolves come towards him, and stand about him on the right hand and on the left, himself in the midst: and he stood motionless, saying, 'God, look to my help: Lord, make haste to help me.' They came nearer, and their muzzles touched his clothes: and while he stood unshaken, they turned and left him there unterrified, and on to their ranging of the wood.

So, this assay of his endurance past and he secure, he took his road through the forest. He had not gone far when he heard voices, a gang of Swabian robbers who at that time haunted that countryside: and he heard them go by, prowling in the wood. And so, his constancy again assayed, he defied disaster. But whether this had been a diabolic illusion, or whether it had indeed happened, he could not tell.

Another time he left his cell, and penetrating deeper into these vast solitudes, came upon a monstrous rock, its flanks broken into cliffs and its back jagged with points of rock, untrodden by man: and there he spied a secret hollow cave. He came up closer, to examine the hiding place, and found inside the cave a bear's den, and the bear himself within. He bade the wild creature to go gently away, nor hereafter, said he, return to this mountain pass again. And the bear went gently away, nor ever dared return. The place is about seven miles, more or less, from Annegrey. . . .

Yet marvel not that bird and beast should obey

the command of the man of God. For Chamnoald, now in the episcopal purple at Lyons, and once his servant and disciple, is evidence for it: he used to tell that he often saw him when he would have gone walking in the woods to fast or to pray, how he would call the creatures of the wild, birds or beasts, to him, and how they would come at once to his call, and he would stroke them with his hand and caress them: and the wild things and the birds would leap and frisk about him for sheer happiness, jumping up on him as young dogs jump on their masters. Even that small wild creature that men call in the vulgar tongue the squirrel, would come at his call from the high tree-tops, and the saint would take it in his hand and set it on his shoulder, and it would be running in and out of the folds of his cowl: and this the aforesaid bishop said he had often seen.

ST. MALO AND THE SOW

AT one time when he was going up and down through Brittany to sow the seed of the divine word in the field of the husbandry of God, he came upon a swineherd in a meadow, twisted with bitter grief. He had been herding a drove of pigs, and a greedy unmannerly sow among them was destroying a field of standing corn, and he, trying to save his neighbour's crop, had thrown an ill-directed stone at her and killed her. And now he was in dread of his lord's wrath on his offence,

and what he knew would put a keener edge upon
it was the seven piglings trotting about, trying to
draw milk as of old from their dead mother's dugs,
and able to find no stay for their own lives from
that lifeless body. St. Malo, whose heart had room
only for compassion, could not watch the swineherd's tears without tears himself: and pouring out
a prayer to God, he laid his staff on the ear of the
dead sow, and raising her up by that sole touch, he
brought back joy to the mourner. The swineherd
told the story to his master, and had the praises of
the servant of God in every man's mouth. And the
master, mounting his horse, came to give his thanks
to the saint, face to face, and offered one of his
farms to the church, for the use, under him, of the
servants of God.

ST. MALO AND THE WREN

AND another miracle he wrought like to this, worthy of record for its compassion alone. He was a follower of Paul the Apostle, whose own hands supplied his wants, if aught were lacking: and when he had leisure from his task of preaching the Gospel, he kept himself by the work of his hands. One day he was busy with the brethren in the vineyard, pruning the vines, and for better speed in his work took off his cloak and laid it out of sight. When his work was done and he came to take his cloak, he found that the small bird whom common folk call a wren had laid an egg on it. And knowing that God's care is not far from the birds, since not one of them falls on the ground without the Father, he let his cloak lie there, till the eggs were hatched and the wren brought out her brood. And this was the marvel, that all the time that cloak lay there, there fell no rain upon it. And whoever came to hear of it, they glorified the power of God, and they praised God's own pity in man.

ST. CUTHBERT IN THE SHEILING

ONE day as he rode his solitary way about the third hour after sunrise, he came by chance upon a hamlet a spear's cast from the track, and turned off the road to it. The woman of the house that he went into was the pious mother of a family, and he was anxious to rest there a little while, and to ask some provision for the horse that carried him rather than for himself, for it was the oncoming of winter. The woman brought him kindly in, and was earnest with him that he would let her get ready a meal, for his own comfort, but the man of God denied her. 'I must not eat yet,' said he, 'because today is a fast.' It was indeed Friday when the faithful for the most part prolong their fast until the third hour before sunset, for reverence of the Lord's Passion. The woman, full hospitable zeal, insisted. 'See now,' said she, 'the road that you are going, you will find never a clach-an or a single house upon it, and indeed you have a long way yet before you, and you will not be at the end of it before sundown. So do, I ask you, take some food before you go, or you will have to keep your fast the whole day, and maybe even till the morrow.' But though she pressed him hard, devotion to his religion overcame her entreating, and he went through the day fasting, until evening.

But as twilight fell and he began to see that he

could not come to the end of the journey he had planned that day, and that there was no human habitation near where he could stay the night, suddenly as he rode he saw close by a huddle of shepherds' huts, built ramshackle for the summer, and now lying open and deserted. Thither he went in search of shelter, tethered his horse to the inside wall, gathered up a bundle of hay that the wind had torn from the thatch, and set it before him for fodder. Himself had begun to say his hours when suddenly in the midst of his chanting of the Psalms he saw his horse rear up his head and begin cropping the thatch of the hovel and dragging it down, and in the middle of the falling thatch came tumbling a linen cloth lapped up: curious to know what it might be, he finished his prayer, came up and found wrapped in the linen cloth a piece of loaf still hot, and meat, enough for one man's meal. And chanting his thanks for heaven's grace, 'I thank God,' said he, 'Who has stooped to make a feast for me that was fasting for love of His Passion, and for my comrade.' So he divided the piece of loaf that he had found, and gave half to the horse, and the rest he kept for himself to eat, and from that day he was the readier to fasting because he understood that the meal had been prepared for him in the solitude by His gift Who of old fed Elijah the solitary in like fashion by the birds, when there was no man near to minister to him; Whose eyes are on them that fear Him and that hope in His mercy, that He will snatch their souls from death and cherish them in their hunger. And this story I had from a brother of our monastery which is at the mouth of the river Wear, a priest, Ingwald by name, who has the grace of his great age rather to contemplate things eternal with a pure heart than things temporal with the eyes of earth: and he said that he had it from Cuthbert himself, the time that he was Bishop.

ST. CUTHBERT AND THE OTTERS

I T was his way for the most part to wander in those places and to preach in those remote hamlets, perched on steep rugged mountain sides, where other men would have a dread of going, and whose poverty and rude ignorance gave no welcome to any scholar.... Often for a whole week, sometimes for two or three, and even for a full month, he would not return home, but would abide in the mountains, and call these simple folk to heavenly things by his word and his ways....

[*He was, moreover, easily entreated, and came to stay at the abbey of Coldingham on a cliff above the sea.*]

[55]

As was his habit, at night while other men took
their rest, he would go out to pray: and after long
vigils kept far into the night, he would come home
when the hour of common prayer drew near. One
night, a brother of this same monastery saw him go
silently out, and stealthily followed on his track, to
see where he was going or what he would do. And
so he went out from the monastery and, his spy
following him, went down to the sea, above which
the monastery was built: and wading into the
depths till the waves swelled up to his neck and
arms, kept his vigil through the dark with chanting
voiced like the sea. As the twilight of dawn drew
near, he waded back up the beach, and kneeling
there, again began to pray: and as he prayed,
straight from the depths of the sea came two four-
footed beasts which are called by the common
people otters. These, prostrate before him on the
sand, began to busy themselves warming his feet
with pantings, and trying to dry them with their
fur: and when this good office was rendered, and
they had his benediction, they slipped back again
beneath their native waters. He himself returned
home, and sang the hymns of the office with the
brethren at the appointed hour. But the brother
who had stood watching him from the cliffs was
seized with such panic that he could hardly make
his way home, tottering on his feet: and early in the
morning came to him and fell at his feet, begging
forgiveness with his tears for his foolish attempt,

never doubting but that his behaviour of the night was known and discovered.

To whom Cuthbert: 'What ails you, my brother? What have you done? Have you been out and about to try to come at the truth of this night wandering of mine? I forgive you, on this one condition: that you promise to tell no man what you saw, until my death.' . . . And the promise given, he blessed the brother and absolved him alike of the fault and the annoyance his foolish boldness had given: and the brother kept silence on the piece of valour that he had seen, until after the saint's death, when he took pains to tell it to many.

ST. CUTHBERT AND THE RAVENS
ON THE FARNES

SO, in that same monastery [of Lindisfarne] he
fulfilled many years: and at last, with the good
will of his abbot and his brethren to company
him, he set out in deep delight towards that secret
solitude for which he had so long desired and sought
and striven. The coming and going of the active
life had done its long work upon him, and he
rejoiced that now he had earned his right to climb
to the quiet of meditation upon God: happy that he
had at last come in sight of their lot, of whom it is
sung in the Psalms: *They go from strength to
strength: every one of them in Zion appeareth before
God. . . .*

There is an island called Farne, set in the sea –
not like that part of the coast where live the men
of Lindisfarne, which twice a day by the upswel-
ling of the ocean tide (which in Greek is called
rheuma) becomes an island, and twice a day, its
shores again bared by the tide outgoing, is restored
to its neighbour the land – but hidden several
miles to the east of this half-island, and sieged on
this side and on that by the deep and infinite sea.
No man, before God's servant Cuthbert, had been
able to make his dwelling here alone, for the phan-
toms of demons that haunted it: but at the coming
of Christ's soldier, armed with the helmet of sal-

vation, the shield of faith and the sword of the
Spirit which is the word of God, the fiery darts of
the wicked fell quenched, and the foul Enemy himself, with all his satellite mob, was put to fight.

And so Christ's soldier, made by the rout of the
tyrannous host king of this land he had set foot on,
founded a city to match his kingship, and built
houses to match his city. The building was all but
round, measuring from wall to wall about four or
five perches: outside, the wall rose higher than a
standing man: but inside, by cutting away the living
rock, he made it much higher, to the end that all
wantonness of eye and thought constrained and the
whole intent of the mind upreared to high desire,
the holy inhabitant could see nothing from his
dwelling but the sky. This wall he built, not of hewn
stone nor of mortar and brick, but of rough boulders
and turf which he had digged within, and carried:
some of these indeed so huge that one would hardly
think four men could lift them, and yet he is known
to have carried them hither with angelic help and
set them into the wall. He had two houses in his
enclosure, one an oratory, the other a dwelling place
for the common uses of living. The partition walls
he made mostly of plain earth by digging and
hewing within and without; and on them he set a
roof of rough beams and thatch. At the harbour of
the island was a larger house in which the brethren
when they came to visit him could be received and

take their rest, and not far off was a well handy for their occasions. . . .

At first indeed he would accept a scant portion of bread from them, and would drink from his well: but after a while he felt it was more fit that he should live by the work of his own hand, after the example of the Fathers. So he asked them to bring him tools to dig the ground with, and wheat to sow: but the grain that he had sown in spring showed no sign of a crop even by the middle of the summer. So when the brethren as usual were visiting him the man of God said, 'It may be the nature of the soil, or it may be it is not the will of God that any wheat should grow for me in this place: so bring me, I pray you, barley, and perhaps I may raise some harvest from it. But if God will give it no increase, it would be better for me to go back to the community than be supported here on other men's labours.' They brought him the barley, and he committed it to the ground, far past the time of sowing, and past all hope of springing: and soon there appeared an abundant crop. When it began to ripen, then came the birds, and it was who among them should devour the most. So up comes God's good servant, as he would afterwards tell – for many a time, with his benign and joyous regard, he would tell in company some of the things that he himself had won by faith, and so strengthen the faith of his hearers – 'And why,' says he, 'are you touching a crop you did not sow? Or is it, maybe,

that you have more need of it than I? If you have
God's leave, do what He allows you: but if not, be
off, and do no more damage to what is not your
own.' He spoke, and at the first word of command,
the birds were off in a body and come what might
for ever after they contained themselves from any
trespass on his harvests. . . .

And here might be told a miracle done by the
blessed Cuthbert in the fashion of the aforesaid
Father, Benedict, wherein the obedience and
humility of birds puts to shame the obstinacy
and arrogance of men. Upon that island for a great
while back a pair of ravens had had their dwelling:
and one day at their nesting time the man of God
spied them tearing with their beaks at the thatch
on the brethren's hospice of which I have spoken,
and carrying off pieces of it in their bill to build
their nest. He thrust at them gently with his hand,
and bade them give over this damage to the brethren. And when they scoffed at his command, 'In
the name of Jesus Christ,' said he, 'be off with you
as quick as ye may, and never more presume to
abide in the place which ye have spoiled.' And
scarcely had he spoken, when they flew dismally
away.

But toward the end of the third day, one of the
two came back, and finding Christ's servant busy
digging, comes with his wings lamentably trailing
and his head bowed to his feet, and his voice low
and humble, and begs pardon with such signs as

he might: which the good father well understanding, gives him permission to return.

As for the other, leave once obtained, he straight goes off to fetch his mate, and with no tarrying, back they both come, and carrying along with them a suitable present, no less than a good sized hunk of hog's lard such as one greases axles with: many a time thereafter the man of God would show it the brethren who came to see him, and would offer it to grease their shoes, and he would urge on them how obedient and humble men should be, when the proudest of birds made haste with prayers and lamentation and presents to atone for the insult he had given to man. And so, for an example of reformed life to men, these did abide for many years thereafter on that same island, and built their nest, nor ever wrought annoyance upon any.

ST. WERBURGA OF CHESTER AND
THE WILD GEESE

IT was in the city of Chester that the girl Werburga, daughter of Wulfhere, King of Mercia, and Ermenhild ... took her vows, and her goodness shone for many years. The story of one miracle done by her I now shall tell, which made a great stir and was long told about the countryside. She had a farm outside the walls, where the wild geese would come and destroy the standing corn in the fields. The steward in charge of the farm took all shifts to drive them off, but with small success. And so, when he came to wait upon his lady, he added his complaint of them to the other tales he would tell her of the day. 'Go,' said she, 'and shut them all into a house.' The countryman, dumbfounded at the oddness of the command, thought that his lady was jesting: but finding her serious and insistent, went back to the field where he had first spied the miscreants, and bade them, speaking loud and clear, to do their lady's bidding and come after him. Whereupon with one accord they gathered themselves into a flock, and walking with down bent necks after their enemy, were shut up under a roof. On one of them, however, the rustic, with no thought of any to accuse him, made bold to dine.

At dawn came the maid, and after scolding the

birds for pillaging other people's property, bade
them take their flight. But the winged creatures
knew that one of their company was missing: nor
did they lack wit to go circling round their lady's
feet, refusing to budge further, and complaining
as best they could, to excite her compassion. She,
through God's revealing, and convinced that all this
clamour was not without cause, turned her gaze
upon the steward, and divined the theft. She bade
him gather up the bones and bring them to her.
And straightway, at a healing sign from the girl's
hand, skin and flesh began to come upon the bones,
and feathers to fledge upon the skin, till the living
bird, at first with eager hop and soon upon the wing,
launched itself into the air. Nor were the others
slow to follow it, their numbers now complete,
though first they made obeisance to their lady and
deliverer. And so the merits of this maid are told at
Chester, and her miracles extolled. Yet though she
be generous and swift to answer all men's prayers,
yet most gracious is her footfall among the women
and boys, who pray as it might be to a neighbour
and a woman of their own countryside.

ST. BENNO AND THE FROG

IT was often the habit of the man of God to go about the fields in meditation and prayer: and once as he passed by a certain marsh, a talkative frog was croaking in its slimy waters: and lest it should disturb his contemplation, he bade it to be a Seraphian, inasmuch as all the frogs in Seraphus are mute. But when he had gone on a little way, he called to mind the saying in Daniel: '*O ye whales and all that move in the waters, bless ye the Lord. O all ye beasts and cattle, bless ye the Lord.'* And fearing lest the singing of the frogs might perchance be more agreeable to God than his own praying, he again issued his command to them, that they should praise God in their accustomed fashion: and soon the air and the fields were vehement with their conversation.

ST. GODRIC AT FINCHALE

I MYSELF as a small boy saw the great Godric, I a youngster and he an old man, and the high memory of it is sweet in my mind. He was small enough in body, but his spirit had the height of heaven. In youth indeed his hair was black, but in his old age, of an angelic whiteness: a broad fore-head, sparkling eyes, heavy eyebrows that almost met, broad shoulders, a lean body, thin with fasting. . . . He was a monk of Durham, and for sixty years lived a hermit: he died an old man and full of days in his chosen dwelling place in Finchale: and being dead, his virtue speaketh. . . .

Finchale, the place where the man of God accomplished his warfare, was thought to have its name in ancient days from a King called Finc. The sound of this name seems to speak a certain harshness in the British tongue which is unknown in our own. The ancients say that here of old time lived Finc, King of Britain, and that he built greatly here. Indeed, hidden under the green grass are the traces of ruined foundations, and where the ground is digged deeper, the questing spade many a time uncovers the crowding bones of the dead, in the womb of the earth itself. Whence is it plain that here were once the thronging habitations of men, to which this vision of burial places and of foundations is testimony beyond our doubting.

The Wear, a river that is rich and teeming with many kinds of fish, flows round this spot, circling it round on east and north and west: and no part of it is free from the river save the south only. Access to this lap of earth is indeed possible, but it easily escapes the knowledge and the inroads of the chance wayfarer: for on the southern side, by which it is approached, it is hemmed in by the dense shadow of a wood of tall trees, through which at this time there was no track, save only such devious and circuitous ways as the wild creatures use, wandering and cropping here and there through the wood. The place is sunk in a deep valley, and on the further bank, across the river which washes these three sides, great cliffs and mountains hem it in and circle it around: while from these peaks and chasms a shadow falls that grows and lengthens as though itself were a vast mountain. To one who stands below and gazes up, the mountains seem to rise and overhang like giant towers, a beetling height that casts a strange dread upon the heart. Yet below the sweep of their encircling, there lies in the depth of the valley a stretch of level land, shut in by woods of no great height, but very fair, and in this place, beside the flowing of the teeming river, the man of God began to build the tiny habitations of his going out and coming in. . . .

[*At his first coming he had built an oratory, and one day saw above the altar two young and very lovely maids: the one of them, Mary Magdalene, the other the Mother of God: and the Mother of God put her hand upon his head and taught him to sing after her this prayer:*

Mary Holy Virgin, mother of Jesus Christ of
    Nazareth,
Hold, shield and help thy Godric,
Take him, bring him soon to the Kingdom of
    God with thee.]

Thereafter with more devotion than ever he served the Lord: and called upon the most blessed

Mother of God, even as he had promised her, in all
distress that came about him, and found her most
swift to aid. A long time thus spent in solitude, his
friends compelled him to take some one to wait on
him, and have a better care of his outward affairs.
For so intent was he upon prayer, meditation and
contemplation that he would spend no labour on
things out of doors. At first therefore, a little boy,
his brother's son, came to wait upon him, and was
with him for eleven years. At that time the only
living thing he had about him was a single cow:
and because the boy was yet but small and of very
tender years, he would often be so drowsy with
sleep in the mornings that he would forget to take
the beast to pasture, or fetch her again in the eve-
nings: or indeed perhaps the familiar task became
a weariness to him.

So one day the man of God went up to the creature, and putting his girdle about her neck, spoke
to her as if to one that had reason and intelligence.
'Come,' said he, 'follow me, and go on with me to
thy pasture.' She went on, and the youngster, looking and listening, followed after them. And again
the saint spoke. 'I command thee, in the Lord's
name,' said he, 'that every day at sunrise thou shalt
go forth alone, with no guide, to thy pasture; and
every noon and evening at the fitting time, come
home with no servant to lead thee: and when thine
udder with fulness of milk needs easing come to
me, wherever I shall be, and when thou art milked,

go lightened back to thy pasture, if yet there is time.' And, marvel as it is, from that day and thenceforward, the cow went and came at the proper hour, and whenever through the day she was heavy with milk she would come to him: and if by chance he were in church she would stand outside, by the door, lowing and complaining, calling him. And he, his hour of prayer ended, would come out and milk her, and she then go away, wherever he bade her. The boy who saw this, told it: for he grew up, and is now a very old man.

In after days, a little lad came to serve in the house of the man of God, and was set to these outside tasks. And not knowing that the cow was accustomed to obey the saint's command, and finding her one day grazing in the meadow, he began to harry her and prod her with a goad. And she, incensed, turned on the youngster and catching him between her horns, charged off with him in a great heat of indignation, to the door of the house where the man of God was busy within. He came out, took the boy in his arms and lifted him from between her horns, rescuing him unhurt from the wrath of the irate beast.

In this are three works of God which we find singularly admirable: first, that the animal feared to injure or inflict any wound on the servant of her master, but, none the less, by terrifying his boldness and presumption, administered well-deserved punishment: second, that Christ Himself would not have the guileless and ignorant youngster killed, but preserved him by the help of His servant: third, that He made manifest to us the merits of the man of God, in that by his intervention he saved one set amid death from death's very jaws.

This same youngster, now indeed an old man, would often tell the story with thankfulness, praising God who so marvellously deigned to snatch him by the merits of his master from sudden destruction.

ST. GODRIC'S GARDEN AND
THE WILD DEER

NOW if one is intent too long upon one task, the mind in tedium very soon revolts against its undertaking: and so the man of God would turn the energy of his mind to various activities, yet seldom did he suspend his soul from prayer. He had rooted up from the ground near by the unprofitable undergrowth of the wood, and now began upon the tree trunks that were left to graft in cuttings of fruit trees which he had obtained from his visitors, and very skilful he was, and had made for himself a kind of enclosed orchard. In summer, when the tender shoots come to life again with green leaves, the branches he had grafted in began to swell and gradually here and there fragile sprays of green and young leaves appeared. But the unaccustomed sweetness of them was very tempting to the wild things of the wood, and they began very greedily to crop this strange new greenness, and most assiduous they were in visiting this agreeable pasture. They would nip off the sprays of the apple boughs, and gnaw the tender juicy bark and scatter with their hooves the young saplings: and not a single kind of tree, of those he had grafted with so much pains, did these wild creatures of the wood suffer to come to maturity, in their unbridled greed.

So one day coming out of his oratory he saw a

wild stag from the wood cropping the tender leafage of his trees, scattering and spoiling with all its heart: and making his way towards the creature, he bade it with a crook of his finger not to run away from the spot, but to wait till he came, without stirring. Oh strange and stupendous mystery! The stag, this wild thing of the woods, that knew no discretion, understood the will of the man of God from his gesture alone, and standing still it began trembling all over, as if it knew that it had offended the soul of the man of God. Its extreme tremor and fear went to his heart, and he checked the wrath in his mind and the blows he had meant to inflict: and the creature dropped on its knees as he came, and bowed its head, to ask pardon as best it could for its bold trespass. He ungirt his belt, and put it round the neck of the kneeling animal, and so led him beyond the bounds of his orchard, and there releasing him bade him go free wherever he willed. . . .

It was not long after when lo! a herd of the woodland creatures came crowding again: they leapt across the fence, they tore off the tender flowers and delicate leaves, and every one of the slips of apple trees that he had watched over from the beginning and planted or grafted in his garden, they set themselves to root up and break off and trample underfoot. He came out of the house, and ordered the whole mob to leave the place: and seizing a rod, he struck one of them thrice on the flank and leading her to the trees that lay along the ground, he showed her rather by signs than by any spoken word what damage her herd had done to his planting. Then, raising both hand and voice, 'In the name of Jesus of Nazareth,' said he, 'be off and away as quickly as ye may, nor be so bold as to come near this garden of mine to its hurt, until these trees are full-grown: for the slips of fruit trees that I have grafted on these trunks I meant for the food of men and not of beasts.' And so saying, he threatened the rest of the dumb creatures with the rod that he held in his hand. And thereupon the whole herd, with heads down bent and stepping delicately, went out: and where they had rioted prancing here and there and leapt in great bounds, they now went forth stepping as it were on tiptoe, with swift-hurrying hoofs. He drove the whole herd to the depth of the forest: and such as lagged behind in weariness, he set his arms about and gently brought them out, making a way for them by lifting a hurdle from his fence. From that time forth never any forest creature dared to trespass the bounds which he had fixed. . . .

Bears, too, would come from the depth of the forest to eat the honey of his bees, and he would find them out and chastise them with the stick that he always carried in his hand. And at a word from him the unwieldy creatures would roar and run, and creatures that no steel blade could daunt would go in terror of a blow from his light rod.

ST. GODRIC AND ST. JOHN THE
BAPTIST'S SALMON

IT was the serene and joyous weather of high
summer, and the turning of the year brought
nigh the solemn feast of St. John the Baptist.
And because the man of God had begged it, and it
was the familiar custom, two brothers from the
monastery at Durham were sent out to him to celebrate the divine office with all due honour. The
office reverently said, and this most solemn Mass
ended, the folk who had come for the Feast made
their way home; and the brethren came to him
to ask his blessing, and leave to return to their
monastery.

'Ye may have God's blessing,' said he, 'but when
St. Cuthbert's sons have come to visit me, they
must not go home without their dinner': and, calling
his serving-man, 'Quick, beloved,' said he, 'and set
up the table, for these brethren are to eat with us
this day.'

The table was set up, and oat cake laid upon it,
such as he had, and bowls of good milk. Yet when
he looked at the feast, it seemed to him but poor,
and he bade the serving-man bring fish as well.

'Master,' said he in amaze, 'where should we get
fish at a time like this, in all this heat and drought,
when we can see the very bottom of the river? We
can cross dry shod where we used to spread the

seine and the nets.' But he answered, 'Go quickly and spread my seine in that same dry pool.' The man went out and did as he was told: but with no hope of any sort of catch.

He came back, declaring that the pool had dried up till the very sands of it were parched; and his master bade him make haste to fill the cauldron with water, and set it on the hearth to heat, and this was done. After a little while he bade his man go to the bank and bring back his catch: the man went and looked, and came back empty-handed: he did it again a second time: and then in disgust, refused to go any more. For a little while the man of God held his peace, and then spoke. 'Now go this time,' said he, 'for this very hour the fish has come into the net, that St. John the Baptist promised me; for never could he break a promise by not doing what he said, although our sluggish faith deserved it little. And look you,' said he, 'but that salmon that is now caught in the seine is a marvellous fine one.' So in the end his man went off, and found even as he had been told: and drawing it out of the net, he brought the fish alive to where his master sat in the oratory, and laid it at his feet. Then, as he was bidden, he cut it into pieces and put it into the pot now boiling on the hearth, and cooked it well, and brought it and set it before the brethren at table, and well were they fed and mightily amazed. For they marvelled how a fish could come swimming up a river of which the very sands were dry: and, above all, how the man of God, talking with them and sitting in the oratory could have seen, by the revelation of the spirit, the very hour when the fish entered the meshes of the net. To which he made reply, 'St. John the Baptist never deserts his own, but sheds the blessing of his great kindness on those that trust in him.' And so he sent them home, well fed and uplifted at so amazing a miracle: praising and glorifying God, who alone doeth marvels, for all that they had seen and heard.

ST. GODRIC AND THE HARE

HE had planted vegetables to feed poor men, and these a little hare used stealthily to devour. He put up with the damage for a long time: but at last the track of its paws betrayed the person of the delinquent: and he came on the thief in his garden, and as it turned in headlong flight he bade it halt. The poor little creature stopped, and waited in trembling and alarm the arrival of its pursuer. The Saint caught it, struck it with his rod, and binding a bundle of vegetables on its shoulders sent it off, with these words: 'See to it that neither thyself nor any of thy acquaintance come to this place again: nor dare to encroach on what was meant for the need of the poor.' And so it befel. . . .

The gentleness of his heart did not betray itself only in kindness to men, but his wise solicitude watched over the very reptiles and the creatures of the earth. For in winter when all about was frozen stiff in the cold, he would go out barefoot, and if he lighted on any animal helpless with misery of the cold, he would set it under his armpit or in his bosom to warm it. Many a time would the kind soul go spying under the thick hedges or tangled patches of briars, and if haply he found a creature that had lost its way, or cowed with the harshness of the weather, or tired, or half dead, he would recover it with all the healing art he had. . . .

And if anyone in his service had caught a bird or little beast in a snare or a trap or a noose, as soon as he found it he would snatch it from their hands and let it go free in the fields or the glades of the wood. So that many a time they would hide their captive spoils under a corn measure or a basket or some more secret hiding-place still: but even so they could never deceive him or keep it hidden. For often without any telling, and indeed with his serving-man disavowing and protesting, he would go straight to the place where the creatures had been hidden: and while the man would stand by crimson with fear and confusion, he would lift them out and set them free. So, too, hares and other beasts fleeing from the huntsmen he would take in, and house them in his hut: and when the ravagers, their hope frustrated, would be gone, he would send them away to their familiar haunts. Many a time the dumb creatures of the wood would swerve aside from where the huntsmen lay in wait, and take shelter in the safety of his hut: for it may be that by some divine instinct they knew that a sure refuge abided their coming.

ST. GODRIC AND THE HUNTED STAG

IN the time of Rainulf, Bishop of Durham, certain of his household had come out for a day's
hunting, with their hounds, and were following
a stag which they had singled out for its beauty.
The creature, hard pressed by the clamour and the
baying, made for Godric's hermitage, and seemed
by its plaintive cries to beseech his help. The old
man came out, saw the stag shivering and exhausted at his gate, and moved with pity bade it hush
its moans, and opening the door of his hut, let it go
in. The creature dropped at the good father's feet,
but he, feeling that the hunt was coming near, came
out, shut the door behind him and sat down in the
open: while the dogs, vexed at the loss of their
quarry, turned back with a mighty baying upon
their masters. They, none the less, following on the
track of the stag, circled round about the place,
plunging through the well-nigh impenetrable brush-
wood of thorns and briars; and hacking a path with
their blades, came upon the man of God in his poor
rags. They questioned him about the stag: but he
would not be the betrayer of his guest, and he made
prudent answer, 'God knows where he may be.'
They looked at the angelic beauty of his countenance, and in reverence for his holiness, they fell
before him and asked his pardon for their bold
intrusion. Many a time afterwards they would tell

what had befallen them there, and marvel at it, and by their oft telling of it, the thing was kept in memory by those that came after. But the stag kept house with Godric until the evening: and then he let it go free. But for years thereafter it would turn from its way to visit him, and lie at his feet, to show what gratitude it could for its deliverance.

ST. CUTHBERT'S BIRDS AND
BARTHOLOMEW,
THE HERMIT OF FARNE

FROM ancient time long past, this island has been inhabited by certain birds whose name and race miraculously persists. At the time of year for building nests, they gather here. And such gracious gentleness have they learned from the holiness of the place, or rather from those who made the place holy by their way of living there, that they have no shrinking from the handling or the gaze of men. They love quiet, and yet no clamour disturbs them. Their nests are built everywhere. Some brood above their eggs beside the altar. No man presumes to molest them or touch the eggs without leave. . . . And they in turn do harm to no man's store for food. They seek it with their mates upon the waves of the sea. The ducklings, once they are reared, follow behind their mothers who lead the way, and once they have entered their native waters, come no more back to the nest. The mothers too, their mild and gentle way of life forgotten, receive their ancient state and instinct with the sea. This is the high prerogative of the island, which, had it come to the knowledge of the scholars of old time, would have had its fair fame blazoned through the earth.

But at one time it befel, whilst a mother was leading her brood, herself going on before, that one of the youngsters fell down a cleft of a creviced rock. The mother stood by in distress, and let no one doubt but that she was then endowed with human reason. For she forthwith turned about, left her youngsters behind, came to Bartholomew, and began tugging at the hem of his cloak with her beak, as if to say plainly: 'Get up and follow me and give me back my son.' He rose at once for her, thinking that he must be sitting on her nest. But as she kept on tugging more and more, he perceived at last that she was asking something from him that she could not come at by voice. And indeed her action was eloquent, if not her discourse. On she went, she first and he after, till coming to the cliff she pointed to the place with her bill, and gazing at Bartholomew, intimated with what signs she could that he was to peer inside. Coming closer, he saw the duckling with its small wings clinging to the rock, and climbing down he brought it back to its mother, who in high delight seemed by her joyous look to give him thanks. Whereupon she took to the water with her sons, and Bartholomew, dumb with astonishment, went back to his oratory.

THE SAINTS OF IRELAND

ST. CIARAN AND THE NESTING BIRD

THE most blessed Ciaran, bishop, and first begotten of the Saints of Ireland, belonged to the west border of Leinster, which is called Ossory. At the time that he was born, all the folk of Ireland were heathen. His father was called Luaigne, of the nobler of the Ossory clan: his mother Liadain, born in the south of Munster. . . . And Ciaran was born and brought up in Corca Laighde, on Cape Clear Island. And verily God chose him from his mother's womb: for when the name of Christ was not yet heard in Ireland, the austerity of the Christian faith began to spring in him. For his parents wondered, and all who saw him, at the soberness of his mind, the gentleness of his nature, the sweetness of his words, his timely fasting, his wise counsels, and the other qualities that belonged to holy men.

One day on this same Cape Clear Island this first of St. Ciaran's miracles came by God's will to pass. For when he was still a lad, a hawk swept down from the sky upon a small bird brooding on its nest and caught it, before St. Ciaran's eyes, and carried it off in its talons into the air. The lad saw it, and was in sore grief over it, and prayed for the poor captive: and straightway the ravisher came down with his prey, and laid the small bird, mangled and half-dead, before him. But under the pitying gaze of the lad, the hapless creature by God's grace was made whole, to his heart's desire: and before his eyes sat brooding on her nest, happy and unhurt.

ST. CIARAN AND BROTHER FOX
AND BROTHER BADGER

FOR thirty years St. Ciaran lived in Ireland, in holiness and integrity of body and soul, without baptism, for the Irish were yet heathen, as we have already said. Nevertheless, by the inspiration of the Holy Ghost in His holy servant Ciaran, he lived devout and perfect in his ways. And hearing a report of the Christian faith in the city of Rome, he left Ireland, and set out to Rome. And on reaching it, he was baptised, and taught in the Catholic faith: and there he remained for twenty years, reading the Holy Scriptures, and collecting books of them, and earnestly studying ecclesiastical discipline. And the Roman people seeing the wisdom and the prudence, the devotion and the faith of Ciaran, the man of God, ordained him bishop there: and then he was sent to Ireland, his own land. And on the road through Italy there met him St. Patrick, archbishop of all Ireland, and the saints of God met face to face and were glad. St. Patrick was not at this time bishop, but was afterwards ordained by Pope Celestine, and sent to Ireland to preach. For him, although there were saints before him in Ireland, God kept the mastery and all the primacy of Ireland: since for no man before Patrick did the Kings and chiefs of Ireland believe in God.

And Patrick said to Ciaran, 'Go thou to Ireland before me: and make thy way to a well in the heart of Ireland, on the border between the men of the North and the men of the South: it is called Fuaran, the little cold well: and there found thy monastery: for in that place shall thy glory and thy resurrection be.' Then said St. Ciaran, 'The place where that well is, is unknown to me.' And St. Patrick answered him: 'Dear Brother, go thy way secure, and God shall be with thee: and take this bell to be thy fellow-traveller on thy journey. It shall be dumb until thou hast come to the well I have told thee of. And when thou hast come to it, thy bell shall sound a clear note, and ring sweetly. And after thirty years I shall come to thee in that place.' And the two servants of God kissed and blessed one another, and St. Ciaran went on his way towards Ireland, but the blessed Patrick stayed behind in Italy. And from that day St. Ciaran's bell was silent and voice-less until he came to the well of Fuaran, as St. Patrick had foretold.

Now when St. Ciaran was come to Ireland, God guided him to the well of Fuaran, and there the bell of the man of God rang plain and clear, which bell is called Ciaran's *bardan*, and is held in great honour in the town and the whole parish of St. Ciaran. For it is carried through the country to the oath-taking of chieftains, to the defence of the poor, and to the levying of the dues of the monastery of St. Ciaran. The bell was indeed cast for the bishop Germanus, master to St. Patrick. And the well is, as has been said, on the border between the two parts of Ireland, but on the southern side, in Munster, among the clan Hele. And the blessed Ciaran began to live as a hermit there: for the place was a vast solitude and thick with forest. And he built himself a poor cell, that was the beginning of a monastery. And thereafter by God's gift a city grew up, through the grace of St. Ciaran. And all these are called by one name, Sierkieran.

Now at St. Ciaran's first coming to that place, he sat himself down under a tree: and under the shadow of it was a fierce boar. The boar, seeing for the first time the countenance of man, fled in sore terror; and then, made tame by God, he came back to St. Ciaran as though to be his serving-man: and that boar was St. Ciaran's first disciple or monk, as one might say, in that place. For straightway that boar, as the man of God watched, began with great vigour tearing down twigs and grass with his teeth to build him a little cell. At that time there was no one with the saint: he had left his disciples behind him and escaped alone to that solitude. Later on other animals came from their dens in the wilds to St. Ciaran, a fox, and a badger, and a wolf and a deer: and they stayed with him, tame and gentle. And they obeyed the saint's word in all things, as if they had been his monks.

But one day the Fox who was shrewder and wilier than the other animals, stole his abbot's shoes and abandoning his vow, carried them off to his ancient dwelling in the forest: intending to chew them there. Knowing this, the good Father sent another monk or disciple, namely the Badger, into the forest after the Fox, to bring back his brother to his post. So the Badger, being well learned in the woods, at once set out in obedience to his abbot's bidding, and took his way straight to the den of Brother Fox. There finding him about to gnaw his master's slippers, he bit his ears and his tail, and cropped his fur, and forced him to come back with him to his monastery, there to do penance for his theft. And the Fox, necessity driving him, and the Badger with him carrying the shoes none the worse, came about Nones to St. Ciaran in his cell. And the saint said to the Fox, 'Wherefore, brother, didst thou do this ill deed, which it becomes not monks to do? Behold, our water is sweet and free to us, and food is here for us all alike to share. And if thou hadst a longing, as is thy nature, to eat flesh, Almighty God would have made it for thee from the roots of these trees, if we had asked Him.' Then the Fox entreated his forgiveness, and did penance fasting, and would not eat until he was bidden by the saint. And thereafter he lived sociably with the others.

In the end, St. Ciaran's disciples and many others sought him out from all parts in that place: and it was the beginning of a famous monastery. But the aforesaid animals abode there, for the rest of their lives, tame and familiar, for the saint was fain to see them.

ST. MOLING AND THE FOX

THE blessed bishop Moling used to keep animals both wild and tame about him, in honour of their Maker, and they would eat out of his hand. And among these was a fox. Now one day the fox stole a hen that belonged to the brethren and ate it. The brethren brought their complaint, and the man of God scolded the fox and accused him of being perfidious above other animals. The fox, however, seeing his master wroth with him, gazed upon him with solicitude, and made off to a convent of nuns that were under St. Moling's care, captured a hen by guile, and bringing her to his lord, presented her safe and sound. And the saint, smiling, said to him: 'Thou hast offered rapine to atone for theft. Take back this hen to her ladies, and deliver her to them unharmed: and hereafter do thou live without stealing, like the rest of the animals.' Hearing this, the fox took the hen between his teeth and deposited her unharmed in her ladies' cloister. And those who saw so great a marvel wrought in either place, made merry over it and blessed God.

Another time another fox stole a book from the brethren, and carried it off to hide it in one of his earths, intending to come back shortly and gnaw it there. But on his return to the monastery, he was found stealing and eating a honeycomb. Whereupon the brethren laid hold on him and brought him to St. Moling, and accused him of stealing the book. And the holy old man bade the brethren to let him go free. And when he was released, the Saint said to him, 'O wise and crafty one, be off, and bring me back that book unharmed, and quickly.' At that, off went the fox, and hasted to bring the book from his cave, and set it down dry and unharmed before the holy bishop. And then he lay upon the ground before the man of God, as if seeking forgiveness. And the Saint said, 'Get up, you wretch, and fear naught: but never touch a book again.' And the fox got up rejoicing, and fulfilled in marvellous wise the Saint's behest: for not only did he never touch books again, but if any one would show him a book in jest, he took to flight.

ST. BRENDAN AND THE
SEA MONSTERS

AND when the Feast of the blessed Paul the
Apostle, who was slain under Nero, was
come, they were eager to celebrate his high
day with devotion and glory. But while the Abbot
was chanting the office, his voice sweet and ringing,

the brethren said, 'Sing lower, Master; or we shall be shipwrecked. For the water is so clear that we can see to the bottom, and we see innumerable fishes great and fierce, such as never were discovered to human eye before, and if thou dost anger them with thy chanting, we shall perish.'

Then the Abbot upbraided them for fools and laughed a great laugh. 'What,' said he, 'has driven out your faith? Fear naught but the Lord our God, and love Him in fear. Many perils have tried you, but the Lord brought you safely out of them all. There is no danger here. What are ye afraid of?' And turning again, Brendan celebrated Mass more solemnly than before. And thereupon the monsters of the deep began to rise on all sides, and making merry for joy of the Feast, followed after the ship. Yet when the office of the day was ended, they straightway turned back and went their way.

ST. BRENDAN AND THE SEA-CAT

THENCE they sailed to another island, lovely indeed but small, in which there was from old time a whirlpool in which fish might be caught. For the sea withdrawing from it, the creatures of the sea were left behind in it. They went across the island, and found a church built of stone, and in it a venerable old man at his prayers. But wherefore say I an old man? For he seemed rather to be animated bones. And the old man said to them, 'O holy men of God, make haste to flee from this island. For there is a sea-cat here, of old time, inveterate in wiles, that hath grown huge through eating excessively of fish.' Thereupon they turned back in haste to their ship, and abandoned the island.

But lo, behind them they saw that beast swimming through the sea, and it had great eyes like vessels of glass. Thereupon they all fell to prayer, and Brendan said, 'Lord Jesus Christ, hinder thy beast.' And straightway arose another beast from the depths of the sea, and approaching fell to battle with the first: and both went down to the depth of the sea, nor were they further seen. Then they gave thanks to God, and turned back to the old man, to question him as to his way of living and whence he had come. And he said to them, 'We were twelve men from the island of Ireland that came to this

place, seeking the place of our resurrection. Eleven
be dead: and I alone remain, awaiting, O saint of
God, the Host from thy hands. We brought with us
in the ship a cat, a most amiable cat and greatly
loved by us: but he grew to great bulk through the
eating of fish, as I said: yet our Lord Jesus Christ
did not suffer him to harm us.' And then he showed
them the way to the land which they sought: and
receiving the Host at the hands of Brendan, he fell
joyfully asleep in the Lord: and he was buried
beside his companions.

ST. BRENDAN AND THE
WHITE BIRDS

AFTER these things they came to an island that was very fair and filled with flowers in bloom and trees in fruit. And when they sought a harbour where they might enter in, they found on the southern coast of the island a little river of sweet water running into the sea, and there they brought their ship to land. . . . Then Brendan said to his brethren, 'Behold, our Lord Jesus Christ, the good, the merciful, hath given us this place wherein to abide His holy resurrection. My brothers, if we had naught else to restore our bodies, this spring alone would suffice us for meat and drink.'

Now there was above the spring a tree of strange height, covered with birds of dazzling white, so crowded on the tree that scarcely could it be seen by human eyes. And looking upon it the man of God began to ponder within himself what cause had brought so great a multitude of birds together on one tree. And so great was the bewilderment of his thoughts that he prayed with tears for the revealing of the mystery. . . . And even as the man of heavenly desires spoke within himself, behold one of the birds flew from the tree, and its wings rang against the ship, like the chiming of a bell: and perching on the highest part of the prow of the

ship, it began to spread out its wings in token of
inward joy, and to gaze with a placid regard upon
the man of God. And straightway the man of God
knew that the Lord had given heed to his prayer,
and he spoke to the bird. 'Inasmuch,' said he, 'as
thou art God's servant and His messenger, then tell
us whence came ye hither, and by whom was so
mighty a multitude of birds gathered in one place.'

And the bird spoke to him. 'We are,' it said, 'of
that great ruin of the ancient foe, who did not
consent to him wholly. Yet because we consented
in part to his sin, our ruin also befell. For God is
just, and keepeth truth and mercy. And so by His
judgment He sent us to this place, where we know
no other pain than that we cannot see the presence
of God. And so hath He estranged us from the
fellowship of those who stood firm. On the solemn
feasts and on the Sabbaths we take such bodies as
ye see, and abide here, praising our Maker. And
as other spirits who are sent through the divers
regions of the air and the earth, so may we speed
also. Now hast thou with thy brethren been one
year upon thy journey: and six years yet remain.
Where this day thou dost keep the Easter feast,
there shalt thou keep it throughout every year of
thy pilgrimage, and thereafter shalt thou find the
thing that thou hast set in thy heart, the land that
was promised to the saints.' And when the bird had
spoken thus, it raised itself up from the prow, and
took its flight to the rest.

And when the hour of evening drew on, then began all the birds that were on the tree to sing as with one voice, beating their wings and saying, *'Praise waiteth for thee, O Lord, in Sion: and unto thee shall the vow be performed.'* And they continued repeating that verse, for the space of one hour. It seemed to the brethren that the melody and the sound of the wings was like a lament that is sweetly sung. Then said St. Brendan to the brethren, 'Do ye refresh your bodies, for this day have your souls been filled with the heavenly bread.' And when the feast was ended, the brethren began to sing the office: and thereafter they rested in quiet until the third watch of the night. Then the man of God awaking, began to rouse the brethren for the Vigils of the Holy Night. And when he had begun the verse, *'Lord, open thou my lips, and my heart shall show forth thy praise,'* all the birds rang out with voice and wing, singing, *'Praise the Lord, all ye his angels: praise ye him, all his hosts.'* And even as at vespers, they sang for the space of one hour. Then, when dawn brought the ending of the night, they all began to sing, *'And let the beauty of the Lord our God be upon us,'* with equal melody and length of chanting, as had been at Matins. At Tierce they sang this verse: *'Sing praises to God, sing praises: sing praises unto our King, sing praises: sing ye praises with understanding.'* And at Sext they sang, *'Lord, lift up the light of thy countenance upon us, and have mercy upon us.'* At Nones they said, '*Behold how good and how pleasant it is for brethren to dwell together in unity.*' And so day and night the birds sang praises to God. And throughout the octaves of the Feast they continued in the praises of God. . . .

Here then the brethren remained until the Whitsun Feast: for the sweet singing of the birds was their delight and their reviving. . . . But when the octave of the Feast was ended, the Saint bade his brethren to make ready the ship, and fill their vessels with water from the spring. And when all was made ready, came the aforesaid bird in swift flight, and rested on the prow of the ship, and said, as if to comfort them against the perils of the sea: 'Know that where ye held the Lord's Supper, in the year that is past, there in like fashion shall ye be on that same night this year. . . . And after eight months ye shall find an island . . . whereon ye shall celebrate the Lord's Nativity.' And when the bird had foretold these things, it returned to its own place.

Then the brethren began to spread their sails and go out to sea. And the birds were singing as with one voice, saying, '*Hear us, O God of our salvation, who art the confidence of all the ends of the earth, and of them that are afar off upon the sea.*' And so for three months they were borne on the breadth of ocean, and saw nothing beyond sea and sky.

ST. CAINNIC AND THE MICE

ONE Sunday St. Cainnic was lodged on the island of Inish Ubdain: but the mice of that place gnawed his shoes and nibbled them and ate them. And the holy man, when he was aware of their naughtiness, cursed the mice, and cast them out of that island for ever. For all the mice, assembling in a body, according to the word of St. Cainnic, precipitated themselves into the depths of the sea, and mice on that island have not been seen unto this day.

ST. CAINNIC AND THE SEA-BIRDS

ANOTHER time St. Cainnic was lodged one Sunday on another island, called En inish, the Isle of Birds. But the birds on it were garrulous and extremely loquacious, and gave annoyance to the Saint of God. So he rebuked their loquacity, and they obeyed his command, for all the birds got together and set their breasts against the ground, and held their peace, and until the hour of matins on Monday morning they stayed without a movement and without a sound, until the Saint released them by his word.

ST. CAINNIC AND THE STAG

ANOTHER time when St. Cainnic was in hidden retreat in solitude, a stag came to him, and would hold the book steady on his antlers as the saint read on. But one day, startled by a sudden fear, he dashed into flight without the abbot's leave, carrying the book still open on his antlers: but thereafter, like a fugitive monk to his abbot, the book safe and unharmed still open on his antlers, he returned.

ST. KEVIN AND THE COW

WANDERING by himself through lonely places, the blessed Kevin came one day upon a glen set in a hollow of the hills and lovely with running water. For there were two lakes, and clear streams here and there flowing down from the mountains. And he went up the valley to the head of the glen where it narrows; there is a lake there, and the mountains very high above it; it lies at their feet, and they rise from its very verge. This valley used to be called in the Irish Glen De, but now it is called Glen da Lough, that is the glen of the two lakes. And St. Kevin settled himself beside the lake in a hollow tree and lived in these strait quarters for some while. Now and then he would go out to gather a few herbs and eat them, and drink a little water. And so he lived, for many days.

Now a herd from a neighbouring farm (the master's name was Bi), would some days bring his cows to pasture in this valley, where St. Kevin lived a hermit. And God, being minded to show his servant Kevin to men, made a cow from that herd come daily to St. Kevin in his hollow: and it would lick the saint's clothes. And towards evening when she would hear the lowing of the herd returning, sated with green grass and well watered, and the high shouting of the herdsmen driving their beasts, she

would hurry to the front of the herd, content with her own pasture. And every day as the herd made its way from the lap of the mountain into the valley, that cow would steal away from the rest, and come to the man of God. And every day she did as on the first day. And that cow had abundance of milk past belief, from the touch of the garments of the man of God. And the byremen, marvelling at the rich streams of milk from her, spoke of it to the master. And he said to the herdsman, 'Do you know what has come to that cow?' The herd knew nothing of it, and his master said, 'Keep a close eye on her, and see where she gets her good favour from.'

So the next day the herdsman left his charge to the youngsters and himself followed after the cow, wherever she went. And the cow took her wonted track to the hollow tree, in which St. Kevin lived. And the herd, finding her licking the saint's coat, stood agape: and then he fell to threatening the cow, and miscalling the man of God as a country-man might. And the saint was ill-pleased, for he feared that the man would betray his presence there. And then the herdsman drove the beasts home to the byre. But when they had got to the farm, the cows and calves fell into such a frenzy that the mothers did not know their own calves and would have killed them. The herdsman, terri-fied, told his master what he had seen in the valley, and at his bidding, came straight back to St.

Kevin, and fell on his knees and begged God's saint to grant him his forgiveness. The saint adjured him, and he vowed not to betray him: for St. Kevin did not know that the story was already told. The man had his pardon, and was given holy water: and when he sprinkled it on the cows and calves, they recognized one another with the old love between them, and were tame again on the spot. But the fame of St. Kevin was carried over the whole countryside. And it came to the ears of some of the older saints, Eogan and Lochan and Enna, that St. Kevin was in that deserted valley: and they took him away with them, against his will, to his monastery. . . .

ST. KEVIN AND THE WILD BOAR

AND in the end St. Kevin came back to his own country, and began to live in that lonely spot, in the glen of the two lakes, where he had been a hermit in his youth, and where the cow used to come to him, as has been told. For that lonely place had been dear to the blessed Kevin from the beginning. In the lower part of the valley he founded a great monastery, at the meeting of two clear rivers. And many came to him from here and there, and St. Kevin made them monks in that place.... Then St. Kevin commended his monastery to trusty men, and gave to each monk his charge. And himself went out from there alone to the head of the glen, as it might be a mile from the monastery, and built himself a tiny hut in a narrow strip between the mountain and the lake, where the trees grew close and there were clear brooks. And he forbade his monks to bring him food of any kind, nor any to come near him unless for great cause.... And the wild things of the mountains and the woods came and kept him company, and would drink water, like domestic creatures, from his hands....

After seven years, St. Kevin built himself a little oratory of osiers, on the northern margin of the lake, where he might make his daily prayer to God. And there the saint lived, known of none, and fed

on no human food, as we have said. But there came
a day when the huntsman of the King of Leinster,
Brandubh son of Eochaid, of the seed of Enna,
who made a slaughter beyond numbering and sore
destruction in a great war against the northern
provinces of Ireland – and the same Brandubh had
the kingship of many of the Kingdoms of Ireland,
after killing Aed the son of Ainmire, King of Tara
and Inishowen in battle – the huntsman came down
after his hounds into the glen, following a boar: and
the boar made into St. Kevin's oratory, but the
hounds did not go in, but lay on their chests outside,
before the gate. And there was St. Kevin praying
under a tree, and a crowd of birds perched on his
shoulders and his hands, and flitting about him,
singing to the saint of God. The huntsman looked:
and dumbfounded he took his way back with his
hounds, and for the sake of the holy solitary's blessing, let the boar go free. He told the marvel that he
had seen to the King and to all of them. And there
were times that the boughs and the leaves of the
trees would sing sweet songs to St. Kevin, that
the melody of heaven might lighten his sore travail.

ST. KEVIN AND THE ROOKS
OF GLENDALOUGH

COLMAN, son of Carbri, chief of the fourth of the men of northern Leinster, in his youth took to wife a woman of rank, but since their habits did in no way agree, sent her away, and took another in her place. Now the woman thus dismissed was wise and dangerous in magic arts, and being passionate against her husband, Colman the chief, she brought to death all the children of the other by her incantations; for as soon as she heard that a son or daughter had been born to him, she would come from wherever she was to stand over against the dun where the child lay, and sing magic songs, until the little creature was dead. So, when a little son was born to him in his old age, he was straightway baptised, lest he should die through her witchcraft unchristened; and he was called Faoláin. And then the chief his father sent him to St. Kevin, that he might protect him by the strength of God from this woman, and bring him up in the ways of the world. And he offered him to St. Kevin, promising that he and his seed after him should be buried by the house of St. Kevin for ever, and should serve him, if Faoláin should escape alive. And St. Kevin took the child gladly, and brought him up as a layman should be, even as his father had said; and he loved him dearly. But St.

Kevin knew not where to look for new milk to feed the small babe, because women and cows were far from his monastery: and he prayed to God to give him some assistance in the matter. And God sent St. Kevin a doe from the mountain near by, and on her milk the baby Faoláin was reared. Twice a day until the child was grown, the doe would come to St. Kevin's monastery, and there be milked by one of the brethren, and go back in all gentleness to her pasture.

But there came a day when the brother, milking her out of doors, set down the vessel with the milk on the ground: and up came a greedy rook intent upon a drink, and with its beak upset both pail and milk on the ground. And seeing it, St. Kevin spoke to that rook. 'For long enough,' said he, 'shalt thou and thy race do penance for this crime. For on the day of my departure to heaven, there shall be much preparing of beef, and ye shall not eat thereof. And if any one of you make so bold as to touch so much as the blood or the offal of the cattle that shall be slain during those days, he shall die on the spot. And everywhere shall be merrymaking, but ye on the heights of these mountains that stand round us shall be sad, cawing and having the law of one another for very dismalness.' And this marvel is fulfilled every year unto this day, even as the Saint foretold.

THE MOUNTAINS THAT ARE
CREATURES OF GOD

AFTER these things the Angel of God came to St. Kevin, saying, 'O saint of God, God hath sent me to thee, to bring thee to the place which the Lord hath appointed thee, to the east of the lesser lake, and there thou shalt be with thy brethren: for in that place shall thy resurrection be.'

St. Kevin said, 'If it had not displeased my Lord, in this place where I have borne travail for Christ, I would fain have remained until my death.'

Then answered the Angel, 'If thou wilt go with thy monks to this place, there shall be many of the sons of life in it until the end of the world, and when thou art gone thy monks shall have a sufficiency of this world's goods. And many thousands of blessed souls shall rise with thee from that place, to the kingdom of Heaven.'

Said St. Kevin, 'Indeed, O holy messenger, it is not possible for monks to dwell in that valley hemmed in by the mountains, unless God should aid them by His power.'

Then answered the Angel, 'Hear these words, O man of God. Fifty men of thy monks if thou wilt have it so shall God fill with heavenly bread, and naught of earthly sustenance at all, if they remain of one spirit in Christ after thy death: and to each of

them that dies shall another succeed in the fear and
the love of God, in habit and in vow, until the Day
of Judgment.'

Said St. Kevin, 'I like it not that there should be
so few monks after me in that place.'

Then answered the Angel, 'If thou likest it not
that there should be so few in that place, then shall
many thousands live there, without stint or poverty,
God supplying their worldly store, for ever. And
thou from thy heavenly seat shalt rule thy family
on earth, even as thou wilt, in Christ. And by God's
aid, thou shalt rule thy monks here and hereafter.
For this place shall be holy and revered: the kings
and the great ones of Ireland shall make it glorious
to the glory of God because of thee, in lands, in
silver and in gold, in precious stones and silken
raiment, in treasures from over sea, and the delights
of kings, and rich shall be its harvest fields. A great
city shall rise there. And the burial place of thy
monks shall be most sacred, and none that lie
beneath its soil shall know the pains of hell. And
verily if thou shouldst will that these four mountains which close this valley in should be levelled
into rich and gentle meadow lands, beyond question
thy God will do it for thee.'

Said St. Kevin, 'I have no wish that the creatures
of God should be moved because of me: my God
can help that place in some other fashion. And
moreover, all the wild creatures on these mountains
are my house mates, gentle and familiar with me,

and they would be sad of this that thou hast said.'
And in such discourse the Angel of God and St.
Kevin made their way across the waters of the lake.

ST. KEVIN AND THE BLACKBIRD

AT one Lenten season, St. Kevin, as was his way, fled from the company of men to a certain solitude, and in a little hut that did but keep out the sun and the rain, gave himself earnestly to reading and to prayer, and his leisure to contemplation alone. And as he knelt in his accustomed fashion, with his hand outstretched through the window and lifted up to heaven, a blackbird settled on it, and busying herself as in her nest, laid in it an egg. And so moved was the saint that in all patience and gentleness he remained, neither closing nor withdrawing his hand: but until the young ones were fully hatched he held it out unwearied, shaping it for the purpose. And for a sign of perpetual remembrance of this thing, all the images of St. Kevin throughout Ireland show a blackbird in his outstretched hand.

ST. CIARAN OF CLONMACNOISE
AND THE STAG

THE glorious and most saintly abbot Ciaran . . . had his origin from the northern part of Ireland, from the folk of the Ards. . . . He was like a burning lamp, of charity so rare that not only did the fervour and devotion of his pitiful heart go out to the relieving of the hunger of men, but he showed himself tireless in caring for the dumb beasts in their necessity. . . .

Then the blessed Ciaran went out from St. Senan and came to his brethren Luchen and Odran, living in the monastery which is called Isel, that is, the low-lying place: and for a while he lived with them. And his brothers made St. Ciaran their almoner and master of the guest house. Luchen, who was the elder, was abbot of that place, and Odran prior. And at one time, St. Ciaran was reading out of doors in the graveyard in the sun, when he suddenly spied some weary travellers going into the guest house: and hurriedly getting up, he forgot his book, and it lay open out of doors until the morrow. Meantime, as he busied himself settling his guests in their quarters and bathing their feet and eagerly tending them, the night fell. In that same night there fell great rains: but by God's will the open book was found dry and sound: not a drop of rain had fallen upon it, and all the ground round about it was damp. For which St. Ciaran and his brethren gave Christ praise. . . .

One day, when St. Ciaran was working in the field, there came to him a poor man asking for alms. At that very hour a chariot with two horses had been brought in offering to St. Ciaran by a certain lord, the son of Crimthann, King of Connaught: and these horses and chariot gave Ciaran to this poor man. Now St. Ciaran's brothers could not endure the vastness of his charity, for every day he divided their substance among the poor, and so they said to him, 'Brother, depart from us: for we cannot live in the same place with thee and feed and keep our brethren for God, because of thy unbounded lavishness.' To whom St. Ciaran made reply: 'If I had remained in this place, it would not have been Isel (that is, the low-lying): not low but high, but great and honourable.' And with that St. Ciaran blessed his brothers, and taking his wallet with his books on his shoulder, he set out from thence. And when he had gone a little way from the place, there met him on the path a stag, awaiting him in all gentleness: and St. Ciaran set his wallet on his back, and wherever the stag went, the blessed Ciaran followed him. And the stag came to Lough Ree, which is in the east of Connaught, and stood over against Hare Island, which is in that lake. Then St. Ciaran knew that God had called him to that island: and blessing the stag, he sent him away, and went to that island and dwelt there. And the fame of his holiness spread abroad, and from far and near good men came together to him, and St. Ciaran made them his monks. . . .

And one day as they rowed across, St. Ciaran's gospel which a brother was holding carelessly fell into the lake, and for a great while it lay under the waters and was not found. But one summer day the cows came into the lake, to cool themselves in the water from the great heat of the sun: and when they were coming out from it, the leather wallet in which the Gospel had been put had caught about the foot of one of the cows, and so the cow dragged the wallet with her back to dry land: and inside the sodden leather the book of the gospel was found, clean and dry and shining white, with no trace of damp, as if it had been hidden in a library. For which St. Ciaran rejoiced, and his brethren with him. . . .

And after these things came a man of Munster . . . Donnan by name, to St. Ciaran dwelling on Hare Island. And to him one day St. Ciaran said, 'What seek you, my father, in these parts?' And St. Donnan replied, 'Master, I seek a place to abide in, where I may serve Christ in exile.' Then said St. Ciaran, 'Abide, father, in this place: for I shall go to some other: I know that this is not the place of my resurrection.' Then St. Ciaran gave Hare Island with his household goods to St. Donnan, and came to a place called Ard Mantain on the river Shannon: but he would not dwell in that place, and said, 'I

will not to dwell in this place, for here there will
be a great plenty of the things of this world, and
worldly delight: and hard would it be for the souls
of my disciples to go to heaven, if I should live here:
for the place belongs to the men of this world.' And
thereafter St. Ciaran left that place and came to the
place which was called of old Ard Tiprat, but is
now called Clonmacnoise. And coming to the place
he said: 'Here shall I dwell: for many souls shall go
forth from this place to the Kingdom of God: and
in this place shall my resurrection be.' So there the
blessed Ciaran lived with his disciples, and began
to found a great monastery there: and many from
all sides came to him, and his parish spread about
him far: and the name of St. Ciaran was famous
throughout all Ireland. And a famous and holy city
rose in that place to the honour of St. Ciaran, and
its name was Clonmacnoise . . . and in it whether
they be kings or princes, the chiefs of the sons of
Niall and of Connaught are buried beside St.
Ciaran there. . . .

So for one year did our most holy patron saint
Ciaran dwell in his city of Clonmacnoise. And when
he knew that the day of his death was drawing
nigh, he prophesied weeping of the future evils that
would fall after his day upon that place: and said
that their life would be a poor thing. Then said the
brethren: 'Father, what shall we do in the day of
these calamities? Shall we abide here beside thy
relics? Or shall we seek another place?' To whom

St. Ciaran said: 'Haste ye to some other place of peace, and leave my relics as it might be the dry bones of a stag on the mountain. Better for you that your life should be with my spirit in heaven, than that ye should abide dishonoured beside my bones upon earth.' And when the hour of his departing drew nigh he bade them carry him out of doors from the house, and gazing up at the sky said, 'Steep is that road: and it must needs be.' The brethren said to him, 'Father, we know that nothing is hard for thee: but for us feeble folk, there is sore dread in this hour.' And again brought back into the house he lifted up his hand and blessed his people and his clergy, and having received the sacrifice of the Lord, on the ninth day of September he gave up the ghost, in the thirty-third year of his age.

ST. COLMAN AND THE COCK, THE
MOUSE, AND THE FLY

NOW, among the other virtues with which
the Holy Ghost had endowed him, he was
a great lover and keeper of evangelic poverty, and so marvellous a despiser of transitory
things, that he would have no earthly possessions,
nor gifts, nor kept any property of his own at all,
unless you could call property three small creatures
that Ketinus saith he had in friendliness about him,
a Cock, a Mouse, and a Fly. The way that he used
the Cock was that its crowing wakened him at
night to Lauds, as a bell might. But the offices
rendered by the Mouse and the Fly were the
stranger and more remarkable in that these whom
nature has designed to the fret and annoyance of
mankind, the amazing kindness of God directed,
against the weight of nature, to tendance upon His
servants. For this was the service of the Mouse to
the man of God, that it would not allow him to sleep
or lie at peace beyond the fixed hour that he had
laid down for himself in his holy vows: but when
his body and his tired limbs, worn out with vigil
and prayer and his other austerities, would have
craved sleep and rest beyond the stern limits of
his vow, the Mouse, sometimes by gnawing at his
clothes, sometimes by nibbling at his ear, would
drag him from all quiet. Dear was this office to the

man of God, for by it he saw not only his vows fulfilled, but himself provoked by a dumb creature to the service of God.

Yet scarcely less remarkable was the office of the Fly. For when the man of God had leisure to read his holy books, the Fly would trot up and down his codex: and should some one call him, or he had to go about other business, he would instruct the Fly to sit down upon the line at which he had halted, and keep his place until he should return to continue his interrupted reading: which the Fly infallibly would do. Marvellous are these condescensions of the grace of God, and, as one might say, the collusions of Christ with His saints: yet incredible only to those who have too little thought for how marvellous is God in His praises, how gracious and tender His affection for those that sincerely love Him: and how befitting His ineffable loving kindness that those who have renounced all fellowship and service of men that their spirits may be swifter to serve Him, should themselves receive the good offices of dumb beasts, and a kind of human ministering: and the God whose high and tremendous majesty they acknowledge and adore should yet be found by them a benign and most indulgent friend.

And yet it befell, in the ruling of that divine wisdom that in strange vicissitude now takes its favours from the servants of God and now bestows them, now will have them comforted, and now left desolate: it befell, as the aforesaid Ketinus relates,

that these three little creatures died, and their kind
service and company was lost to the man of God.
And in heavy sorrow, he wrote of his loss to the
friend of his spirit, St. Columba, Abbot of Iona, at
that time living in austerity, far from his own land.
And the story goes that in reply St. Columba wrote
at once in jest and in wisdom, that 'there is neither
lack nor loss where neither substance nor property
is found': as though to question why a man of
God, consecrated to supreme renunciation and to
poverty, should set that heart on small things, which
had renounced and spurned great things and high.

SOURCES

The Desert Fathers

Pp. 3, 6. The Hermit's Garden: The Penitent Wolf: Sulpicius Severus, *Dialogus*, I. c. 13, 14. (*Corp. Script. Eccl. Lat.*)

P. 8 The Blessed Ammon: Rufinus, *Historia Monachorum*, c. 8. (Migne, *P.L.* XXI. c. 420–1.)

P. 12. St. Macarius and the Hyæna: from a French translation of the Coptic text by Amélineau, *Monastères de la Basse-Egypte*, 233 ff.

P. 15. St. Pachome and the Crocodiles: *Vita S. Pachomii* (translated by Dionysius Exiguus), c. 17, 19. (Migne, *P.L.* LXXIII. c. 240 ff.)

P. 17. The Abbot Helenus and the Wild Ass: Rufinus, *op. cit.* c. 11.

P. 18. The Abbot Helenus and the Crocodile: Palladius, *Historia Lausiaca*, c. 59. (Migne, *P.L.* LXXIII. c. 1167.)

P. 20. St. Simeon Stylites: *Vita* by Antonius his disciple, c. X. (Migne, *P.L.* LXXIII. c. 330.)

P. 22. The Unsociable Lion: *Verba Seniorum* (translated from the Greek of an unknown author by John the Subdeacon in the sixth century), II. c. 15. (Migne, *P.L.* LXXIII. c. 1003.)

P. 23. The Abbot Gerasimus and the Lion: John Moschus, *Pratum Spirituale*, c. 107. (Migne, *P.L.* LXXIV. c. 172 ff.)

P. 27. St. Jerome and the Lion and the Donkey: *Vita Divi Hieronymi*. (Migne, *P.L.* XXII. c. 209 ff.)

The Saints of the West

P. 37. The Death of King Teudiric: *Book of Llan Dâv* (edited by J. G. Evans and J. Rhys), p. 141.

P. 40. St. Columba and the Crane: Adamnan, *Vita S. Columbae* (ed. J. T. Fowler), I. c. 48.

P. 42. St. Columba and the White Horse: *op. cit.* III. c. 23.

P. 46. St. Columban in the Vosges: Jonas, *Vita S. Columbani*, c. 15, 30. (Migne, *P.L.* LXXXVII. c. 1020, 1028.)

Pp. 49, 51. St. Malo and the Sow: St. Malo and the Wren: Sigebert of Gembloux, *Vita S. Maclovii*, c. 14, 15. (Migne, *P.L.* CLX, c. 738 ff.)

BEASTS AND SAINTS

Pp. 52, 55, 58.   St. Cuthbert: Bede, *De Vita et Miraculis S. Cudberti*, c. 5; 9, 10; 17, 19, 20. (*Pat. Ecc. Ang. Bede, IV.*)

P. 63.   St. Werburga and the Wild Geese: William of Malmesbury, *Gesta Pontificum*, IV. 172. (*Chronicles and Memorials.*)

P. 65.   St. Benno and the Frog: *Vita* by Emser, c. 54. *Acta Sanctorum, Jun.* 16. (IV. 139.)

Pp. 73, 76, 79, 82.   *St Godric*. The first paragraph of reminiscence, the bears, the hare, and the hunted stag, are from the *Vita* by Geoffrey, monk of Durham, *Acta Sanctorum*, Mai. 21. The remainder is from the more ornate *Libellus de Vita. . . . S. Godrici*, by his contemporary Reginald, also of Durham (Surtees Society): cap. 22, 51, 52, 39, 71.

P. 84.   St. Cuthbert's Birds and Bartholomew: from the *Vita* by Geoffrey, c. 24, 25, in the appendix to the *Historia Dunelmensis Ecclesiae* by Symeon of Durham. (*Chronicles and Memorials.*)

The Saints in Ireland

Pp. 89, 91, 96, 98, 100, 102, 106, 107, 108, 109, 113, 116, 118. The texts will be found in Plummer's *Vitae Sanctorum Hiberniae* (Oxford, 1910), under the titles of the various saints. *St. Brendan and the Sea Monsters* is from the *Vita Secunda* in the Appendix to Vol. II.

P. 121.   St. Kevin and the Blackbird: Giraldus Cambrensis, *Topographia Hibernica*, II. 28. (*Opera*, ed. Brewer, v. 116.)

P. 127.   St. Colman and the Cock, the Mouse, and the Fly: Colgan, *Vitae Sanctorum . . . Hiberniae*, I. 244a.